Dedication:

With God, all things are possible, including the ability to bring people together to do such an incredible task.

This book is dedicated to the extraordinary women who gave their time, talents and stories to make this work! They are truly amazing, and I wish the utmost success and prosperity in their lives, family and business.

Always and forever, to my incredible husband and son, who allow me to do what I do with support, love, and encouragement.

<u>**The Am**</u>azing <u>**Con**</u>tributing **Boss** *Ladies*

Sherika M. Stroud

Te'Ara Arman

Nadia Francois

Monica Baker

Sherry Davis

Melanie Jones-Williams

Sirnollia Beasley

Michele Sutton

Temycka Carpenter Carlton

"*Lipstick Stories* is more than just a book: it's about giving a voice to women and a shoulder to others to learn from the trials, tribulations and the triumphs of those who are doing the same thing, sister girl, you're not alone…"

Sherika M Stroud

Author, Businessowner, Wife, Mother

Back to Ground Floor
By: Sherry Davis

It's a cloudy, stormy Sunday, and Sherry is sitting on the bed thinking about her dream business. How she was groomed for this opportunity and filled with a passion for fashion. As a child, Sherry watched her parents create and grow their mobile boutique into a business named "Steppin' Up," known across the Upstate of South Carolina. Her parents have always been "two of a kind." Her mom's presence could stop a room. Sherry was named after her mom but only dreamed of having her beauty. Her mom's passion for fashion could not be missed, and her dad had always been the breath of confidence that walks beside her. Watching and helping her parents growing up, Sherry's passion continued to grow for fashion.

Sherry would travel around the Upstate with her parents helping with Steppin' Up. Flashbacks of watching her mom work with all different types of women. Women lined up to get a chance to get the Steppin' Up experience. Her mom, the beauty of the room with style to kill, always found a way to give her clients that special feeling of confidence. This woman with the beautiful hazel eyes helps other women behold the beauty of their own. Memories of watching her mom take fashion to a new level to help other women find inner beauty. She used clothing to complement the beauty they truly held.

With tear-stained cheeks, Sherry sat remembering the love she has for mom and the things that her mom taught her Those sweet memories brought back the understanding of why she fell in love with fashion. She was taught that fashion does more than just turn heads. Fashion gives confidence, and it really accessorizes the true beauty of a woman. Through fashion, helping women love themselves again and hold their heads proud, her mom taught her the importance of giving confidence to women and allowing them to love themselves for who they are.

Knowing that she had to get up and start her day, Sherry couldn't help but wonder how she got to this path in life. And on this path, life felt so challenging. Wondering how she decided she was up for the challenge in the first place. Why did it all look like a dream to outsiders, but felt so normal to her? The realistic version of where she sat didn't come easy and some of the daily challenges were hard.

Watching the rain hit the window so naturally but in unplanned patterns, she looked and thought about her choices. How the entrepreneur spirit seems so natural to her but called for so many unplanned paths in her life. Paths that would cause most people to say, this is too much. The feeling of carrying the world on your back but needing the strength of carrying it with a smile as if the weight is nonexistence. How the word "no" only made her work harder. Why is being what society considered normal so hard for her?

Sherry followed all the "proper" roads to success in life. Exceeding expectations in school, she received her Bachelor of Science degree in Accounting from Clemson University in 2003. Throughout her years of Undergrad at Clemson, fashion was always her favorite pastime. Opportunities to help style her friends always came around, giving everyone advice on how to highlight their good assets, and explaining how to downplay the assets that they wanted to hide. Fashion has always found a place in Sherry's life, even when she tried to put it in the backseat.

Working in the corporate world, she didn't realize that fashion was not always welcomed. The fact that her fashion became a distraction for others brought about disdaining looks that halted her daily fashion looks. Instead, she tried to fit into the corporate box of expectations. She worked full-time in the corporate world and used her evenings and weekends to pursue her determination to make an impression on the fashion world.

Throughout her corporate career, Sherry always found a way to feed that entrepreneurial spirit. She started out selling Avon, and over time got more creative. Personalized photo jewelry was the next venture, and that lead to making hand-made fashion jewelry. From hand-made jewelry to jewelry by the dozens, that fashion spirit started to regrow. Boutique Two Fourteen was born in 2013.

Every name has a meaning, and that meaning provides motivation in your business. The "Boutique" is obvious, but the "Two Fourteen" represents a few things. First, Sherry's daughter was born on Valentine's Day, February 14th. This is the day is all about love, and Boutique Two Fourteen is all about promoting self-love.

Boutique Two Fourteen stands for a woman's identity and loving who you are. All women have layers that show at different times. Two Fourteen has different layers of fashion that can convert and represent the different layers of a woman. Loving one's true self and accessorizing your confidence is a movement of Two Fourteen.

The whole timeline of the birth and growth of Boutique Two Fourteen played out in her head as if she was watching a movie on fast forward speed…

As the business's reputation grew, Sherry thought back to how she became more comfortable in running her business. After all, this was her true passion. It's what she was groomed to do, fashion is what was taught since she was big enough to understand. Then her mom was diagnosed with Esophageal cancer in 2015. When the doctor said it was cancer, Sherry could remember the sharp stab that made her heart stop. The replay of that day still makes her heart bleed like the doctor was saying it all over again. Trying hard to comprehend and stand strong, her family just held each other harder. They were determined that this thing was not going to break their chain. Then instantly, Boutique Two Fourteen began to mean even more to her and her family. This boutique was a point of strength for her mom. To see her joy of helping with the boutique is a memory that Sherry still cherishes. Even going through her chemo treatment, her mom never once lost her beauty or sense of fashion. To see her mom, stand strong and face cancer gave Sherry more strength to push for Boutique Two Fourteen's success.

Sherry began to regularly set up at a local salon, and eventually settled into that location. She thinks back to her budget at the time and says, "Thank God they were willing to work with me on the rental fee!" Things were going well; people were starting to realize where Two Fourteen was located. She was a woman on a mission and was determined to do it all. Working a regular corporate job, building a real estate business and a boutique business. Thinking back to the people that were willing to be a part of her dream. Her younger cousin was always volunteering her time to work at the boutique and go out to vending events. One of her best friends saw that she was in need of help and asked her what she could do to help. She dedicated her time to help her grow the boutique, and never required an on-going regular salary. Working alongside her, they began to make plans for the boutique growth and what the future opportunities would bring. She agreed to be the boutique manager, which allowed Sherry more time to focus on her mom and real estate clients. The stress of the day-to-day obligations of the boutique was no longer a worry because it was now being properly managed. Sherry trusted this woman with her life, so trusting her with the boutique didn't feel like an issue at all.

Sherry's first cousin volunteered to step up and help out with the boutique as well. She became Boutique Two Fourteen's personal stylist. Her taste is always on point with the current trends, and she never missed a beat when things were out of place. Things were going great! Both of her businesses were going in the right direction, her mom's treatment was going well, and she was working my way out of corporate.

Sherry created a website, boutique Two Fourteen.com, to share what the boutique had to offer to the world. Boutique Two Fourteen would not be just local, they wanted the boutique to reach around the globe.

Boutique Two Fourteen was in its first fashion show ever thanks to the boutique's manager. The manager reached out to the organizer, and Two Fourteen was in the show. The manager worked to organize the boutique's portion in the show, and the stylist got to work with styling the models. Things were tense during the time leading up to the show. The night of the show, Two Fourteen was a showstopper. Sherry smiles as this was one of the highlights of being a boutique owner. Everyone enjoyed the show, but Sherry's inspirations were missing. Her parents couldn't come to the fashion show because her mom wasn't feeling well. But she knew that her mom was there with her in spirit, so she pushed on. A tear dropped as she thought about how hurt she was not to be by her mom's side that night. Being the owner, her presence was required at the show. Most people never even knew that the big smile that night was to hide the growing pain of wanting to breakdown and cry. Joy and sadness collide, but only smiles were shown in appreciation of the boutique's models, her team, and the opportunity to be part of the show.

After the show, a dark cloud loomed over the team at the boutique. What was seen to be the dream team, was slowly being torn apart? Somehow friendships of a lifetime were being destroyed; she lost her manager in the fallout. Still unsure of how it all happened, so many unanswered questions, how did she lose her childhood best friend to some made-up drama? None the less, Sherry had to accept the split and swallow the hurt. Out of personal belief, she does not participate in drama, and business has no room for it. And the pain felt from the loss of that close relationship still stings.

Losing her manager, she leaned on her stylist and her daughter even more. They were always up to the challenge of helping. Thanks to unnecessary drama, the boutique took a hit. Right during growth came the valley. But failure was not part of the plan, Boutique Two Fourteen kept pushing for success. Things did slow down because the dedicated time was no longer there. The focus was more on standing strong for her mom. But the team continued to make plans for the boutique. Sherry and her mom had laid out plans for the boutique once she beat cancer's ass. Things were going steady for the boutique.

Then a few months later, Sherry got a call that caught her off guard. It was the call stating that her current location situation was not working out for everyone involved. They had to make a business decision, and the space dedicated to the boutique could no longer continue as planned. And just like that, the business took another blow. Many assumed that the news was going to bring about an ugly response, but she held her head high. She understood that they had to do what they felt was right for their business too. Business is business, and personal feelings are not always important. Sherry's boutique now had no location and nobody to run the day-to-day operations. What was a girl to do? One thing in life, not just business, we must understand is that everything happens for a reason.

Natasha, Sherry's cousin, stopped her and told her something that she needed to hear. She said "The boutique will be there. Take this time to cherish your mom. She needs you more than anyone else right now." Those words stuck and allowed her to regain focus on what was important in life. Without the demands on her time to be at the boutique, she was able to focus more on her mom, daughter, and the rest of her family. These are the people that needed her love and attention way more than the boutique at the time. Taking a break from the boutique allowed her to enjoy and create memories that she would get to hold onto for a lifetime. Memories that she would have missed without that very important short conversation with her cousin. Sherry realized that she didn't have to let the boutique go but allowing it to be on the backburner was okay.

While walking down the small Main St. of Fountain Inn with her daughter she walked into a place that allowed a variety of vendors to set up long term. After speaking with the owner, it was decided to set up a pop-up shop inside of her location. The agreement didn't require her to be present during all open hours. Funds were collected from customers and disbursed to her weekly. This sounded like the match she had been waiting for. The ability to have a presence in the marketplace, but the freedom to continue to stay focused on family first. Dates were decided upon and all was well. The excitement gave her boutique the adjustment that it was needing at the time.

Then the most devastating thing happened. Sherry's mom's battle with cancer ended, and she walked into Glory on September 24 of 2017. The reality was crushing, to say the least. She was on autopilot and was lost beneath the mask. The energy level was low, and everything was emotional. Sherry's world was broken, and she was realizing that nothing could fix it. Stuck between anger and sorrow, there was no true focus on the horizon to get things in order to set up the long-term pop-up shop. Anyone that studied her face could see the tear stains down her cheeks. Lost and confused, Sherry thought how she was supposed to move forward without the support of her mom. The world she knew no longer existed.

Weeks passed and she slowly started adjusting to not being able to get up and speak with her mom. The thoughts of hearing her mom telling her, "do what you need to do, I'm ok," played over and over in her head. Sherry was finally able to admit she needed to work on getting her business moving in the right direction again. Determined to succeed, despite the crying in silent spaces, she began to work on getting everything set up at the pop-up location.

Sherry was determined not to give up. Her mind knew people were watching and waiting for her world to fall apart. People watched and wondered and finally started to ask, "how do you do it?" Sherry simply gave a response that "I have to." Some people would simply say, "I'm proud of you because I could not do it." Those people meant well, but it only made it hurt worse. She didn't know herself how she was moving forward. She simply knew there were no other options. Her living hero was now in Glory, and she didn't know how to put the puzzle together but knew she had to work on the puzzle daily. She just prayed everything would not come tumbling down. Her mom, her hero, taught her to Smile through the storms, Trust in God, that's the only option sometimes to make it through. Sherry prayed some days every hour asking for strength. She would ask God, "how is it fair for you to take my mom away from me." Daily, she looked up in the sky to tell her mom "hey beautiful." She knew her angel was watching her. And she was determined to keep her legend alive and building. Every day was a new day to try again to make her and her mom's dreams come true. Even in spirit, the inspiration of her mom pushed her forward.

Mid-October of 2017, Boutique Two Fourteen was officially in its new pop-up location. New location in a new town, time to bring in a new client base. Even though not required, Sherry made time to be onsite to meet new people and introduce herself to the community. There were new people looking for different styles and trying to find somewhere that they could shop for their style. The other vendors at the location were really nice and welcoming to her. As time went on, Sherry realized that the location was not a good fit for her business. Nice location on Main St, but her items were not displayed to bring in new customers and space did not accommodate the needs of her customers for a fitting room. A decision had to be made, move to a different location or stop again.

With that burning entrepreneurial spirit, Sherry sought out to find a new location. Trying to decide where in the Upstate of SC should she pick for her first location. After a couple of months of debating, she finally found a building that seems to suit the boutique's needs. Several conversations later, an agreement was met with the property manager. The lease was signed, and it was time to put in the work. The excitement was unreal, Boutique Two Fourteen would finally have a home of its own. Time to put in the work.

Getting the boutique ready for opening day was a lot of fun. With the help of her family, the shop was prepared for business. The weeks spent preparing for opening the boutique created sweet family memories that they would always remember. Like how paper purchased to cover the windows had fiberglass in it and it caused her dad and her fiancé to itch like crazy. The walls were painted a bright blue with neon pink for the trim. Repairs were made to the dressing room floor, plumbing work in the bathrooms, weather stripping the back door, and the worklist goes on. The process was hard, but it was rewarding. Sherry did all that she could to keep the boutique opening and location quiet. She didn't want everyone to know she was working on the biggest move yet for her business.

Opening day came, and the team was still preparing the boutique for presentation. Clothes were being overnighted for delivery, and final repairs were being made. Her family and close friends pitched in to create a special day for Boutique Two Fourteen. Sherry felt so much pride standing in her family's very own boutique. As this has always been a family dream, that the congratulations weren't just to her. Congratulations were due to everyone that put in the hard work to make to possible. Everyone that dedicated some of their time to the growth of Boutique Two Fourteen. The grand opening went great, and Sherry was ecstatic.

Two Fourteen was up and running, and Sherry had to return to the corporate world. She was so grateful for the dedication of her fiancé to help her follow her dreams. He agreed to run the boutique while Sherry was at work and running for her real estate clients. Everything was going great; the boutique was picking up more clientele as the weeks following. The rush was still there, but the pressure was there also. Decisions on the clothes to wear, the best way to advertise, and finding ways to promote the boutique to potential customers.

Then one day out of an attempt to push Sherry out of the corporate world, her fiancé told her that he would not perform any of the duties that came along with running the boutique. The management of the boutique rested solely in her hands. She needed to understand that she could not do both. He ended the conversation by stating, "You cannot have both worlds, it's your dream or theirs." The conversation was in comparison to a papercut. He didn't cause a bleed out, but the pain of the news cut deep. How did she misunderstand the help that he was willing to offer? His intentions were good but the pressure to be independent always caused a pause in her willingness to walk away from the corporate world.

Summer was gone, fall was fading, and winter was knocking the door down. With winter setting in, the temperature in the boutique felt just like the temp outside. Nothing they did kept the boutique warm enough for comfort. Eventually, the days spent at the boutique lessened and hours got shortened. Property management stated that they would handle the issue, but the repairs never came. Too busy running for real estate clients and working in corporate business, Sherry didn't have the time to properly deal with all the issues and business needs of the boutique.

Working and managing a boutique brought great pride, but just as much work went on behind the scenes of the boutique. She was working hard to hold on to her dream, and not to be discouraged in the midst of the battle.

Over the next couple of months, it got harder to keep the passion behind fighting for the boutique. Sherry could feel the difference in her approach and cried at night as her dream was slipping away. She would ask herself why am I really pushing to have this business? Do I still have a passion for this fashion world? Am I making a difference with my push for fashion? The answers to the questions were scrambled like a crossword puzzle, and Sherry couldn't figure out how to formulate the words to give a logical answer.

Eventually, there were no more open days of Boutique Two Fourteen. Two Fourteen was fading away three times faster than the rate of its growth. Even though all the bills were paid on time, the rest of the work needed was lagging. She felt lost and there was nobody that could find her. She could not find the passion to pick up the pieces. The pain of this reality was killing her on the inside, but she kept smiling for everyone watching.

The final days of the boutique consisted of cleaning out and final sales. While smiling on the outside, Sherry was truly saddened on the inside. Her dream seemed to come alive and die right before her eyes.

The sound of thunder and lightning snapped Sherry out of her trance of the short movie, "The story of Boutique Two Fourteen". The sheer sound of her cries and vision of her tears was enough to make her know that it was her reality. Now she sat staring through the waterfalls in her eyes, faced with decisions only she can make. Does she walk away from the whole dream? Could she truly make a difference and leave her mark on the industry with her vision? Did she fully process the thought of having her business before? Could she adjust and produce a healthy balance in her business? Was the passion lost for a little while or completely gone?

This was a day of realization and pure pain. She had to figure out how to deal with her inner wounds. Part of the pain was the reality that her role model, her mom, was no longer in this world. Learning to deal with the grief had to be part of the process. She understood that passion started the fading process when she lost her mom. The pain was so real that she could not understand why her mom could not be sitting beside her rubbing her back saying, "Baby, it's going to be alright." Who said it was okay to take her mom from her? She had so much to learn from her and discover with her. Sherry just shook her head because she couldn't figure out how to overcome but knew that this is not what her mom would want.

So, she stood up with a brush of love as if her mom was still there, wiped her eyes, and said "This is the point of change. Time to stand up to the world and be ready to fight for success again." She stared in the mirror and begin to ask herself what happened to you? Why did you allow things out of your control to change your love and passion? Time to stand in your shoes again and be who you loved to be, not what the world loves. As days went on, she started to realize that the clothing and routines she possessed had nothing resembling a boutique. Sherry realized her first step back to her passion was through herself. She forgot the very thing Two Fourteen stood for, where was her self-love?

It was time to face that she is not superwoman. Her potential and aspirations may scream superpowers, but reality said she is only one person. After she gets herself together, it will be time to build a team. Finding someone to mentor and groom to run the day today. She has that passionate love affair with fashion, but her drive didn't allow her to do all the things required by herself.

It was time to start planning and properly creating goals for Boutique Two Fourteen. Sherry started to creating a notebook of ideas to grow the business. She was becoming re-energized to follow that passion for fashion again.

She was back on the ground floor of this journey, but this time she brought more to the table. The experience and lessons learned would be worth more in the future than she ever realized. She smiled and said, "The blessing is in the lesson."

<u>**Notes from the Author**</u>

Hey everybody!

Thank you for reading my story! This tale is based on my journey of being a business owner. I'm excited about sharing my story with the following businesswomen determined to be successful. I have been quiet about my story for a long time because I feared the conversations. But I'm learning to live in my truth and love me!

I went through a lot of trials along my journey, but I understand that everybody's journey is different. Understand that every journey is different and never compare your journey to someone else's. You will never know the complete story of their journey to understand what their sacrifices were or who helped them along the way. Be clear that success starts with a dream and potential that leads to planning and comes full circle with the work invested. There will be people to help along the way, and it's okay if you didn't do it by yourself.

A couple of key things:

1. Make sure the passions that lead to your business always have a presence.

2. Plan accordingly and accept challenges.

3. You might have to do everything yourself mentally, but the reality is a different story.

4. Learn to delegate to ensure that your business is run smoothly.

5. Never adjust your dream for other people's intentions.

I hope that I have inspired someone!

Finding your Passion

By Sirnollia Beasley-Wilson

My name is Sirnollia Beasley. I grew up in the suburbs in Montgomery, IL. My parents had 3 kids and I am the second to the oldest child. I graduated from Oswego High School in 1998.

Right after High School I attended college and took up Graphic Design. While I was attending College of DuPage I started working as a receptionist at Photography by Feltes. One day on my way to work there was a guy parked in my spot. I ignored it. A few more days go by and it is the same person parking in my spot. One day I noticed after school (college) he was following me from the college campus to my job. Once I got to work, I told Jack (owner) that I feel that someone is stalking me, and I refuse to go to the front desk. Jack checked it out. He saw someone in their car but never got out. I told Jack that was him. Jack went outside and asked him; "How can I help you? Are you lost?". The person told Jack no he does not need any help. Jack told him that this property is for his customers who are taking their pictures. The stalker said ok and left the property. The next day I was at the campus in the food court and long and behold the stalker was right beside me.

He came and took it upon himself to sit at my table. He told me that he does not know how to ask this but wanted to know if I would go out to dinner with him that weekend. Of course, I told him to know. It was freaky that he was stalking me. He got up and walked away. The weekend was finally here, but I had to work that Saturday morning. Long and behold he was waiting in the parking. I went up to his car and said; "What do you want"? He said; "I am not leaving here until I get a date with you. I told him fine only if he stops with the stalking. I pick the place. He said fine.

So, we went on our first date together. As we got to know each other he said what are you doing next Friday night? I asked why. He said because I have a friend who is having a party at his house and I believe you guys would be great for each other. I said "REALLY". I chuckled and said I would need to think about it. He said no, really, I think you guys would be great. Bring a few friends. He calls his friend and said hey, I have someone that I want you to meet. She will be coming over to your next Friday. He said cool, bring her over.

The following Friday night rolls around. My girlfriends and I are getting ready to go to this house party. My friend and I followed the stalker over to the house in North Aurora, IL. We walked into the house and it was a room full of people. I went over to the kitchen opened the fridge because I was looking for something to drink and this person said who are you? I said very rudely who are you? He said I am the person who owns this house. I said yea right you are too young to own this house. If this is YOUR HOUSE, your parents must be away on business or just out of town. He said I own this house; I will show you. Long and behold he showed me the title. I was floored. So, from that night on we started dating.

I got pregnant with our first child. Our first child was born in April of 2000. My boyfriend and I were not seeing much of each other because my parents were determined to make sure that I finished college. With both of my parents working my grandma (on my dad's side of the family) came over and lived with us until I graduated from the College of DuPage and got my Associates Degree. Since I was the first one to graduate college a lot of my relatives including my parents wanted me to further my education and get my bachelor's. Why? The higher the degree the better they pay. Believe it or not, I was able to graduate with my bachelor's degree only because my other grandma (on my mom's side) took the train back and forth every other day and watched my firstborn. In 2002 I finally graduated from Robert Morris College.

I was told after graduation through Robert Morris College that I would have a steady job in the Graphic Design industry. Well, that did not go so well. Every application I submitted told me that they are looking for someone who has 5 years or more experience to work as a Graphic Designer. How are you supposed to get the experience, and NO ONE hires you!

Having a child at the age of 20, I had to have some type of money coming in. I am now trying to figure out my future in my career because the graphic design was just not happening. I was able to get a job as a telemarketer for Controlled F.O.R.C.E. It was like God was on my side that day. I did not interview at all for the position. I saw the job opportunity in the newspaper. I went to Batavia, IL the next morning. Once I got there, I saw a young lady answering the phones and doing mailings. I told her I was there to get an application to fill out. She said we can do that later when can you start, I have a good feeling about you. I said I can start now. So, on my first day, I was answering phones and stuffing envelopes. A few hours later she said come here I want to introduce you to a couple of people. We went to the back of the office and she told the owner "You need to add her to payroll, she just started working here today". The owner said "ok". I will get her information by the end of the day. I never interviewed for this job. Then the next person this young lady introduced me too I found out was her father. He asked me what I went to school for and just welcomed me aboard. Working at Controlled F.O.R.C.E. (small business) taught me a lot. Diana (owner) taught me phone skills and customer service, etc.

In the meantime, while I was working at Controlled F.O.R.C.E. a realtor was doing appraisals in North Aurora, IL. She stopped by my boyfriend's house and asked if she can do an appraisal. He said sure. She loved his house and said that if he finished the basement, we can get more money out of it. She told us that an outlet mall is being built a few miles from us, so that is why the value of the homes will be going up. Sure enough, back in the fall of 2002, the Chicago Premium Outlet Mall was built. We took her advice and rehab our home for $10,000. We sold our home and profited $173,000. Not bad for our first paycheck. So, my boyfriend was up late one-night watching infomercials and ended up purchasing Carleton H. Sheets's real estate investing course. By taking his course we ended up using his strategies to buy a townhome in 2001 with the money we made off our home. Our thought process behind this was we will live in the home, rehab them and turn around and sell them. From 2001-2007 we have profited $502,000 from real estate investing. We used our cash to purchase the home and rehab them.

As far as my career went, I left Controlled F.O.R.C.E. in 2004 and started working for Crate & Barrel. By working there, I was able to learn more about customer service which has helped me a lot.

In 2006 my boyfriend and I had a second child. Due to the Real Estate Investing taking off the way it did I was able to leave Crate & Barrel in November of 2006 to be a stay at home mom for both of my boys. Besides, my entire paycheck was going to daycare.

In 2007 I realized that this was a business and we needed to start acting like one. My boyfriend and I opened our first business together in September of 2007. The name of the business was called "Wilson's American

Dream Investments". Before the market crashed in 2008 our company made $3.2 million. However, because we were young and making the money no one took the time and took us under their wings to properly show us how to manage our money.

Real Estate Investing was our bread and butter. That was our only source of income. In 2008 when the market crashed, we were doing ok, but not great like before. I have noticed the change when our offers to purchase homes were not getting accepted anymore. I would put in 100 offers a day. I was getting nervous because we planned on getting married in June of 2009. We decided to seek out some answers on what we were going to do with our business. Our money was slowly going down to keep up with our lifestyle. The last profit we made in 2009 was $64,000. In 2009 we spent out $30,000 in another real estate guru program. They promised us that they can assist to get our offers accepted. That did not pan out as it should have. We ended up shutting our doors in 2010.

In 2010 I entered back into the W2 land. Going from temp agency to temp agency to make ends meet. In 2012 I landed a position with Draper & Kramer as a receptionist and moved up to becoming a leasing agent. Working for Draper and Kramer and becoming a leasing agent taught me a lot about property management. I did enjoy myself working there but started noticing how much I missed taking vacations whenever I wanted, spending quality time with my boys, etc. I was itching to get back into the Real Estate Investing Game. Due to my working as a leasing agent with Draper & Kramer, one of the benefits was renting an apartment through them. Now, keep in mind that I am the only one working and trying to rebuild my credit, so I did not think that we should have moved out of my parent's house. My husband was so persistent that he wanted out of my parents' home and wanted me to speak with my property manager on which apartment homes were available for leasing agents. Of course, I was going to choose the lowest rent possible, because I wanted to rebuild my credit with the commissions that I was making at the time. Did that happen…NO. Of course, he had to choose the most expensive one we had. With his interior design mindset, he could not see himself live in an apartment that was not fully updated to his standards. We could have had a 2-bedroom apartment for $500 a month and that was with my discount. That was not good enough. He wanted the largest 2 bedrooms we had (1200 sq. ft.) and with my discount, it was $1400 month. Mind you that we were barely making it. I was the only one working at the time. I had to cover rent, utilities, food, gas, phone bills, kids' activities, etc. all off one income. I had to increase my income and real estate was the only way I knew how.

In the fall of 2013, I came across a yellow bandit sign about real estate investing. I called the number on the sign and let me tell you it was the best decision of my life. This group taught me about multiple streams of income, how to create and build wealth and even protect my legacy. This was the first time I entered the world of network marketing. I was super pumped because in my mind EVERYONE needs to know about how to minimize their taxes, start a business, fix their credit, create and build wealth, etc. Was going to the classes to learn only was not implementing anything yet. I wanted this to be a joint effort, but my husband had no interest. He kept telling me that this was a scam.

From 2010 to this very day my husband was going through a deep depression. He was unable to provide for his family the way that he did back in 1998. Due to me getting back into the workforce and implementing what I was learning through the real estate class, he felt I was moving too fast. He could not keep up with me and had no desire to do so. His depression leads to drugs and alcohol. He refused to get a 9-5. He has always been self-employed his entire life. He knows what he was worth and refused to work for anybody who paid him for less. Unfortunately, due to all the negativity, my husband and I ended up separating in February of 2014.

So, now being a single mother of two boys I had to make ends meet. This time I wanted to start building and creating my wealth the correct way. I had a checklist on what needed to be done to slowly restart building a solid financial foundation. So, my job in 2015 was to enroll students in the program on how to invest in real estate. To just enroll 1 student into the lowest program my commission would be $1,000. To enroll 1 student in the highest program my commission would be $10,000. That right there would have helped our money situation a lot. So, I opened my business called Beasley's Dynamic Enterprises in April of 2015. I just knew I was going to make some money.

I was determined to make one sale a month. That would have brought home an extra $1,000. I dedicated 3 years to the Real Estate Investing Group. I made sure that I was there every Thursday evening and every other Saturday. I was not coming home until 2:00 in the morning on most nights. Let me tell you all the dedication and money I put into this I did not learn how to to get leads. You were on your own. I was able to get leads by handwriting bandit signs and putting them out late at night on the weekends. I did get leads through that but the leads that were calling in would not buy. I was stumped. I prayed and I prayed why people were not buying. In the fall of 2016, I was watching this person on periscope. I really loved what she was talking about. I took her up on her offer and she started to become my financial coach. As I am talking out loud with her, she asked me one simple question. How much is the program? I said: "On the low end it is ONLY $2,000". She told me in this economy most people can not afford the $2,000 even with the down payment you offer, because they don't see it as an investment. They see it as another DEBT. That is when the lights came on and realized that I needed to go back and teach the basics of money 101.

So, in 2017 I got into another network marketing program thinking that I was going to do well with them because it is teaching basic financial literacy. Nope, that did not go well either. No one who I was marketing too had no interest. They all told me that they were comfortable where they are. So now what? Three years in business and still NO INCOME.

In the fall of 2016, I went to class one day for real estate investing. One of the instructors that day blew my mind about Family Banking and how you can become your banker. I took it upon myself to learn more and meet my instructor's mentor in Alabama in February of 2017. I was blown away on how much life insurance has improved. I spent the rest of the year learning more. In August of 2018, I ended up getting my life insurance license. As I am getting older and seeing my elders and the other ones around me, I started to realize that this economy that we live in is getting worse. Unfortunately, we can not rely on the government for anything, especially for our retirement. We need to learn how to keep more of our income.

What I am learning about in our economy is beyond amazing. I started to realize that each insurance product serves differently. We all have different goals and dreams. God did not make us the same. I take pride in protecting my clients from the two worst market corrections since the Great Depression and I make it my goal to ease the financial concerns my clients face on their journey to their retirement destination. I now know how important it is to find the right blend of growth and safety that is unique to each of my clients. I focus now on two main goals: making sure my clients know the importance of protecting their principal investment and utilizing a unique three-step process to plan to protect and preserve retirement assets and help clients reach their retirement destination.

With the right coaches in place now I have learned my target audience. Yes, it took me 4 years to find out who my target is and how to brand myself and best of all where my passion lies. Any business you open please make sure you follow the process and don't rush. The right people will come, and the money will follow. As business owners, we are always investing in ourselves. Never give up.

THE YELLOW BRICK ROAD TO YOUR DESTINATION

By: Monica Baker

There it is, glistening, golden and beckoning you to take the first step. You've watched as many set off on their journey, while you contemplate how to take the next step. The stories of those that tried and failed come to mind as you push your fears aside, take a step and then a leap of faith and start out on the yellow brick road to your destination.

The road to entrepreneurship is never a straightforward path. There will be many curves, snares and mountains to climb as you navigate your way through the steps needed to build a business that will stand the test of time, let alone the first year. The most important step of all is taking the first step.

My desire to own a business started around age 16. I watched from the sidelines as my grandparents enjoyed the freedom of self-employment. My maternal grandfather Henry ran multiple businesses, from hauling and recycling junk steel to auto repair and owning multiple real estate investments. My paternal grandmother Mildred ran a cleaning and catering service. What they both had in common was the ability to control their lives and the freedom from having to answer to a boss (although Papa Henry still had to answer to the house boss grandma Norma). Being an entrepreneur was etched in my mind and so I set out as a bright-eyed teenager, ready to start my own business.

My best-friend KK also wanted to start a business, so we became partners. The business we chose was transferring photos to VHS tapes. She researched the equipment that we would need to complete the job and then we came up with a plan on how to raise funds. Next, we headed to our local Kinkos print shop to print up business flyers. Over the next week, we went door-to-door handing out flyers. After the last flyer was gone, we patiently waited for our first customer. As the days turned into weeks, we soon realized that those customers would never come. Much to our disappointment, our new business had closed before it had even started. Not only did we experience the close of business, but also the loss of capital from buying flyers and the time spent passing them out. That early experience was one that I would carry with me as I opened and closed numerous businesses along my entrepreneurial journey.

My journey has been one of ups and downs, trials and triumphs. It often reminds me of the story of *The Wizard of Oz* (Baum, 1939). Just as Dorothy and her friends each had desires which motivated them to journey to Oz, my desire of becoming a full-time entrepreneur has been my driving force. But just like Dorothy and her friends, the road to get there has been a series of twists, turns, and rocky roads. The journey of becoming an entrepreneur will always present hardships along the way, but the motivation to reach your destination is the driving force to keep you moving forward. For me, that driving force has been having a clear vision, passion and a lot of determination.

The pathway to success starts with having a vision. A vision to an entrepreneur is like a blueprint to an architect. Your vision IS your destination and every entrepreneur must determine what it is and how to get there.

Until I became clear on MY vision, I realized that I was on a spinning wheel to nowhere. For the better part of 10 years, I had opened and closed multiple businesses, chasing after the opportunity of someone else's vision. I had signed up with numerous direct sales companies, hoping to sell enough products to make a decent income, but barely breaking even. My story ended like many others; exhaustion from chasing down customers that promised but never fulfilled, growing debt from monthly auto-shipments and thousands of dollars of unsold inventory waiting to hit the expiration date before the trash bin. I didn't blame my lack of success on any company in particular, but it was hard for me to follow a scripted blueprint that I didn't believe in. If I didn't believe the script, why should I expect my customers to? While watching the debt grow from my opportunities, there were many times that I considered just throwing in the entrepreneurial towel altogether and sticking to my 9-5, but there was something in my spirit that would not allow me to succumb. It was then that I realized I needed to become clear on MY vision and find the blueprint to what I believed in. I never once imagined that my opportunity would come in the form of an online boutique, but after taking a course on how to create products and post them for sale, I had finally found my opportunity and Eden's Queens was born.

When I started Eden's Queens, my vision was to create an Afrocentric boutique for merchandise that was empowering, inspiring and uplifting. With the tagline "Every Queen Knows Her Worth" I wanted to bring home the message that as African American women we must always hold our heads up and wear our crowns. I wanted a shop that celebrated our old school classy values, while also being proud of our heritage, our hair and whatever else society said we should be ashamed of. I wanted to showcase products that promoted love and unity and to bring unique items for African American women to the marketplace in an era where big companies have been disrespectful to our demographic and our commerce. I wanted to be a part of a growing movement of African American creators, designers, and merchandisers that were promoting cultural positivity, unity, and self-love.

I remember getting a review from a customer that had purchased one of my tote bags that had positive words printed all over it. She loved the bold and descriptive words that described a Melanin Queen and she shared that my products were what she had been searching for. That review was a confirmation to my vision, a vision that has been the driving force to my passion.

When I think about passion, I envision it as the fuel that keeps you going, even when doubt starts to kick in. Being passionate allows you to sell yourself and your business to others. If you are not passionate and don't believe in your business, how can you expect anyone else to? Being passionate about your business means that you are never too afraid or fearful to talk about what it is that you do. You are more than happy to promote your business, even in a sea of no's because you love it and believe in it. When you are passionate, you keep going even if no one else appears to be paying attention. You do it because you know there is someone out there who will eventually connect with your message. Without passion, your opportunity will feel like just another job.

When I first opened Eden's Queens, I created a catalog of products that I thought would sell. I checked my store platform daily and sometimes even multiple times a day, waiting for the first sale. I started working with designers to improve the aesthetics of my designs. I put more money into my business, and I continued to learn from the "pros" on how to run a successful e-commerce store. While it all looked good on the outside, I still had not made any sales. Days turned into weeks which turned into months and I started to wonder if I would have to close yet another business. It reminded me of when I was 16 and waited for the non-existent customers of my first business. I refused to lose, so I continued creating products because I believed in my work and what I had to offer to the marketplace and society. I concluded that if no one else supported my business, I would wear my own products and become my own biggest cheerleader until someone took notice. My passion led me to continue building my catalog of designs, and then one morning it happened. As I was preparing to awake for my 9-5 in the wee hours of the morning, I heard an unfamiliar but pleasant sound coming from my cell phone. It was a loud "Ca-Ching". I didn't really know what it meant, so I logged onto my sales platform and there it was, "Congratulations, you made your 1St sale". I was so excited that I was finally in business. I was excited that someone believed in me. Like magic, I began to hear the sound almost daily, as it was the holiday season. I thought that I was finally on my way, but as quickly as the holidays came and went, so did my sales. I was back to the e-commerce slump. Instead of feeling defeated, I decided to go harder because my passion fueled my determination to grow my vision and continue my journey down the yellow brick road to my destination.

Having a vision and the passion to see it through is great, but it takes a lot of determination to keep everything moving forward. Have you ever tried and failed multiple times, but just kept going? That is because your determination kicked in. My determination started with writing out the steps that I needed to get results. Before doing this, I was grabbing at straws without any real plan. I would sit around and wait for sales, run a few ads and reinvest the revenue back into my business. My business was moving at a snail's pace. I then realized that I needed to create a plan on how to move my business forward. The first step was to write out the goals that I needed to achieve and a time frame for achieving them. I wrote down everything that needed to be done to reach major milestones for my business. I wanted to make sure that my I's were dotted, and my t's were crossed. A few of my goals were to clean up my financial files, organize my design files and create a professional roadmap for my business. Once I listed out all my goals, I created a checklist and timeline. This was what I needed to keep my business moving forward because without a written plan, I found it easy to get off track.

Staying the course can sometimes be a challenge, especially for new entrepreneurs. Just like Dorothy and her venture into the Poppy fields or her dealings with negative forces, many entrepreneurs will have their own Poppy field experience. This can present itself in the form of negativity, self-doubt, procrastination or even unforeseen problems with customers that go along with being a business owner. Some of the negative forces that will present themselves come in the form of naysayers that make you second guess your business, friends or family that do not support your business or even your 9-5 that seems to suck the life right out of you, leaving very little energy and desire to work on your own business. Let's not forget about all the new opportunities (those lovely poppies) that will pop up and try to steal your attention away from your blueprint. The ones where the next guru promises to get you to your destination faster with their "can't live without a course" for the low price of another charge to your credit card. You pay the cost, get started and then after the poppy effect wears off, leave the unfinished course parked somewhere deep in your email account until you remember that you still need to finish it along with the numerous others that are vying for your attention. This is a common experience that I was not immune to but knew that I had to get it all under control. The first commitment that I made was to finish everything that I had purchased before buying anything else. I also committed to pushing aside any negative feelings. I stopped looking for people to support my business and just focused on putting the best product that I could into the marketplace. I also became more self-sufficient by learning new skills that would add value to my business. I remember coming up with a great design of a theme that was currently trending, and I sent the design over to one of my designers and asked for a quote to create the design. The designer told me to give her my budget, which I did, and then she told me to increase my budget. I already knew what the cost of creating the design should be, so instead of increasing my budget, I increased my skill set. After 2 weeks, and a lot of googling and YouTube videos, I created the design myself, along with multiple versions that I could sell. I also learned during my research how to do some of the tasks that I had previously outsourced, which ended up saving my business a lot of money. I had taken control of my business, removed myself from the fog of the poppy fields and continued down the yellow brick road to my destination.

With everything that goes into being an entrepreneur, having a good support system is invaluable. Even Dorothy had her squad, including little Toto. Your support can be your family, your customers, or your business coach. For Eden's Queens, my support system has been a huge part of getting me down the yellow brick road. It is a joy when my family tells me that my new designs are on point, or my customers leave positive reviews about how my products make them feel. Even having a good coach that will provide timely and valuable information to help you continue to grow and push you towards success is invaluable. As you start to see all the pieces fit together and your destination is in close sight, you know that all of your hard work and dedication will not have been in vain. You can see your Oz peeking at you just over the hilltop.

When the time comes that you have arrived at your destination, you realize that it is just the beginning because as an entrepreneur you will continue to evolve and grow. The close of one chapter will be the start of a new one and a new set of blueprints for your next destination. As a new entrepreneur in the e-commerce world, my first year has been an exciting yet challenging ride. As I head into my second year of business, my vision has become even greater. My vision is to open and manage multiple stores, with millions of customers and sales off the charts because no dream is too big on the journey to your destination.

<u>Reference</u>

Langley, N., Garland, J., Morgan, F., LeRoy, M., Ryerson, F., Haley, J., Bolger, R., ...Baum, L. F. (1939). *The Wizard of Oz*. Hollywood, Calif.: Metro Goldwyn Mayer.

From Entrepreneur to Mompreneur: Overcoming the Struggle

By Nadia Francois

My struggle of motherhood mixed with entrepreneurship is one that many women go through as they strive to fulfill their dreams of business ownership. I hope that my story will inspire at least one woman to push through adversity no matter how dim it looks, there is a bright light at the end of the tunnel. I am very faith-centered and in tune with God's plan for my life and I encourage anyone looking to do great things to do the same.

I started in entrepreneurship at a very young age. To be honest, back then I didn't know that this would be my destiny. At the age of 19, I started my first business. It was called Uniforms and more. I sold medical scrubs from the trunk of my car. I kept it going for about 6 or 7 months until my inventory ran out and I couldn't afford to replenish my stock. Back to be an employee and a broke college student but that wasn't the end of my entrepreneurial journey. Enrolled in nursing school as a fulltime student I was on my third job and almost out the door of that one. I couldn't seem to pass a required Chemistry class and time was ticking so I decided to transfer to a school that did not require Chemistry. Little did I know that those plans would go way left. During the change of schools, I met my future husband and father of my children. We dated for about 6 months falling extremely hard for each other.

One year later, we received the news that we had twin boys on the way, a bittersweet moment because my plans of becoming a nurse were once again put on hold but for a wonderful reason. I never thought that I would be a mother, let alone to twins however I embraced it and looked forward to the birth of my little men. Three months after giving birth to the twins we were married, a brand-new life, new goals, and new aspirations to look forward to. Shortly after the wedding, I found out I was pregnant again. This was devastating to me because I already had two babies and was suffering from postpartum depression. My twins were born premature and had to remain in the NICU for 4 weeks after their birth so that separation took a toll on my mental status. The addition of another baby was scary and had me wondering how we would make it when my husband was working a mediocre job and I had not finished school. I prayed and sought counsel from God my father and He told me, "everything you need is in your hands". I struggled with this for a while then I realized what He meant. In my early teens, I would style hair from my mother's kitchen. It was mainly my friends and family, but they were all satisfied, and it paid well. Thinking back on what started as a hustle, God was telling me to use my talents. So, I began to research cosmetology schools in my area and started applying to them. Confirmation of this decision came when I was accepted into a school and given a full scholarship from the local JTPA office. Schooling paid in full, I committed to studying, practicing and passing my state board exams. Not only did I graduate and pass my licensing exams, but I also earned my barber license as well. I opened my own barber salon and business was booming.

Shortly after opening my salon my family life had fallen apart. I had dealt with infidelity issues with my husband in the past but at this point in my life, it was completely unacceptable. I soon confronted him, and we split up shortly after. He abandoned us physically and financially. I suddenly became a single mom. I was now the breadwinner and the babysitter, but GOD had positioned me right where I needed to be. I felt like such a failure because my relationship was over, and I had to raise the boys alone. At this point, I had four sons ages 6 (twins), 5 and 1. I went into deep prayer mode searching for peace and understanding. As I reflected on my life as a wife, mother, entrepreneur, etc. I realized that I was not at peace but just going through the motions to please everyone else. After a few years of self-destructing behavior, trying to drown the pain from the separation, I had lost a lot of my clients and friends. I went through so much grief and anger, very emotional time in my life. I had my talk with God, and he told me to focus on raising my kids pleasing to Him and He would do the rest, and that's just what I did. I took my kids to church, prayed over them and if I couldn't go, I sent them with others. I was still running my business and taking care of them on my own. I was able to bring my kids to work with me if I had to, leave to attend their school programs and extra-curricular activities, and maintain my clientele to keep the funds rolling in. God was doing his part. When I lacked, my family stepped up to help me in any way that they could. We received no child support or visits from their father for years. My hands were taking care of us. God was keeping his promise, so I had to keep mine. The struggle was so real. I couldn't do anything leisure unless someone treated me. Some days we lived off noodles and cereal, but we were never hungry or in the dark.

My salon business boomed for a while, then the recession hit. Business went down to nothing swiftly and I was once again forced to enter the workforce. I was blessed to be able to work in my industry at a local cosmetology school as an administrator. This along with my struggles in the salon-inspired me to go back to school and pursue my degree in Business Administration. I wanted to know all I could about starting, running, and maintaining a successful business. The boys were growing up but still very needy so being employed helped bring some structure along with a steady income. I worked at the school for a little over a year then I was back to be a full-time entrepreneur. This time I looked forward to being fully self-employed especially being enrolled in business school. I was able to implement the things I learned in school into my own business. I also realized that a background in business was very beneficial to the beauty business. The scope of business that is taught in cosmetology school is not thorough enough for novice business owners and in this industry, we graduate as business owners. Over the years I had plenty of side hustles and hobbies, but I was now equipped to own businesses.

My quest as a serial entrepreneur started in my salon as I added products and services that would boost my income. My struggle in single parenting and having no outlet led me to start a nonprofit to empower women and youth in the community. I and four of my clients were in the shop on a Friday night talking about our struggles as women and mothers and Sisters of Empowerment, Inc. was born. We began host empowering events for women that encourages and educates them on current issues, entrepreneurship and mentoring. I then ventured off into the transportation industry starting my own non-emergency medical transportation company, Legacy Transportation. This business was very new to me, but I caught on quick and the money began to roll in. The boys were always my team and worked very hard to help me maintain this business. I ran this office from my salon employing several drivers over the years. I was the backup chauffeur when I didn't have a driver. We made it work. My boys washed the vans, gassed the vans and even did billing to keep our business going. This was the business that was to be passed down to them but due to increased insurance rates and other issues within the industry, I decided to close. Of course, under the counsel of my Father, this decision was made. He told me that I would still have the desires of my heart and I would not have to stress, worry or wonder how. So, I began to re-evaluate my life and what I wanted for my future and it became very clear that I was to use my knowledge to help others build successful businesses. I had been giving out free advice and helping others for years, so it was inevitable that I get paid to do so. I still had the passion to contribute to the beauty industry, the one that raised me, so the Entrepreneur Activity Workbook was published. This workbook assists business owners in the planning stages of their business and the steps ultimately come together and provide a working business plan for their business.

Here are some of my favorite Bible verses that helped to keep me on track and focused on God's promises for my life and overcoming my struggles:

Jeremiah 29:11(NIV)," For I know the plans I have for you," declares the Lord, "plans to prosper you and not to harm you, plans to give you hope and a future."

This scripture tells me that in my mother's wound that there was a purpose for my life. God put me here for a reason and that everything that I go through is a part of that purpose, not to harm me, and that the blessing is in the lesson. We all have trials and tribulations in our lives but those are necessary to mold us into the person God wants us to be. Gracefully broken…

Isaiah 43:2 (NIV), "When you pass through the waters, I will be with you and when you pass through them, they will not sweep over you. When you walk through the fire, you will not be burned; the flames will not set you ablaze."

This scripture tells me that God has me no matter what I'm going through. Sometimes we get caught up in the what and forget about the why. There is a reason that we go through what we go through that's why it is important to stay focused on God.

Isaiah 54:17(NKJV), "No weapon formed against you shall prosper, and every tongue which rises against you in judgment You shall condemn. This is the heritage of the servants of the Lord, and their righteousness is from Me' says the Lord.

This scripture tells me that any negative or evil thing that comes my way is already defeated. That judgment does not belong to man, but God.

1 John 1:9(NKJV), "But if we confess our sins to him, he is faithful and just to forgive us our sins and cleanse us from all wickedness.

This scripture tells me that I am forgiven for all the sins I have committed. All I must do is confess and ask God to forgive me and I will have a fresh start. God is a forgiving God.

Deuteronomy 31:8(NKJV), "And the Lord, He is the one who goes before you. He will be with you, He will not leave you nor forsake you, do not fear or be dismayed.

This scripture tells me to not be afraid to go after what I want in life because God has already made a way for me to achieve it and he will be with me along the way.

The struggles of motherhood mixed with entrepreneurship can extend past some of the circumstances I have had to overcome. My story is a testimony of Faith, Resilience, and Grace that intends to empower all Mompreneurs.

- "Self-Empowerment Leads To Freedom Independence & Excellence "

Te'Ara Arman
Speaker | Mentor | Youth Development | Entrepreneur

DARE! LIVE! BE!

By: Te'Ara Arman

As a woman we have many negatives stacked against us which is what makes us stronger and guides us to success. That success begins when we "Dare to be different". As we are being different, we are stepping out of the cookie-cutter path and taking chances to create our own. Of course, this means we may stand alone at times as we develop and grow into a successful woman who "Live to Inspire" others to believe and invest in themselves to do the same. With the investment, vulnerability is shown, and you get to "Be exactly who you are".

Dare to Be Different

"Do not be conformed to this world, but be transformed by the renewal of your mind, that by testing you may discern what is the will of God, what is good and acceptable and perfect." Romans 12:2

Dare is defined as having the courage necessary. I want you to take five minutes to think about what the word Dare means to you. For me, dare means to step out on faith and take a chance. Looking back over the last five years, I know that I am finally walking in my purpose. So much has gone on and came about for me and my family where the foundation was first put in place back in August 2014.

It was the beginning of the new school year and we had just gotten out of a training class when I was approached by the Director of a Youth Development and Education Program. After approaching me, the Director explained that he was adding a girl's Mentoring group to his program and he would love for me to join his staff alongside another woman as a CO-Facilitator for the group. The Director explained that the way I cared for and educated our youth was phenomenal and he knew that I would add value, be a great Mentor and Asset for the program. As we continued discussing the position and group in detail, I ultimately decided to take the Director up on his offer, which began a new chapter in my life. Over the next couple of weeks, I and the other Facilitator for the girl's group got to know each other and strategized on how we would facilitate the curriculum. We began that group with open minds and a promise to never give up on any of the young ladies.

A girl's group with open communication to discuss anything from a bad grade, traumatic experiences, life skills, conflict resolution, future goals, etc. So, you know we had our challenges and struggles but that is what made the group so successful. I remember having a young lady who tried her best to push away from us because she was uncomfortable with the positive support, love, care, and reinforcement she was receiving. Never received it before, she didn't know how to accept it. She would try to runaway assuming no one would come after her because that's what she was used to. Although, we changed the narrative, went after her and brought her back to shower her with the love, care, and support she deserved. Taking it a step further we showed her how to be that same type of support for her group sisters.

The next couple of months proved to be very rewarding for the young ladies in the group, the facilitators and for the Youth Development and Education Program itself as the ladies were receptive to the help we were giving. During that time, I noticed that although our group was a success, we were just one piece of the Youth Development and Education program. There were several other pieces that needed to be brought together, organized and streamlined for the program to succeed. Impressed by the immediate success of the girl's group, the Director offered me an Interim Executive Director position to run the day to day operations of the program.

Yep, that's right! I became the Interim Executive Director for the Youth Development and Education program alongside my Co-Facilitator role. See the newly appointed position was given as a trial basis to see if I really had what it took to take the program to the next level and boy did I. What the Director didn't know was that one of my life long dreams was to have my own Youth Organization and I not only knew how to run the day to day operations, but I could also organize and plan strategically, develop and implement fundraising strategies, curriculum, student and parenting workshops. I also became the Secretary for the Board of Directors of the Parent company to the Youth Development and Education program. Now I had several titles to add to my resume, an Educator, Co-Facilitator, an Interim Executive Director and Board Secretary. With all of this going on, you can imagine my time was very valuable but the one person that stayed in my corner was my then-boyfriend turned Fiancé by Christmas 2014. So excited and elated, my Fiancé ended my year just right. There were so many people in my ear and environment telling me I was taking on too much and I couldn't accomplish anything with having my hands in so much, but what those people didn't know was I have always Dared to be different, I was on a mission and wasn't about to stop now.

By January 2015, I had officially been named the Executive Director of the Youth and Development Education program and the Board Secretary for the parent company. At this time, I created a new Board Packet and helped conduct a Board Member search for new leaders to help take the organization to new heights. With this process, I began networking outside of the organization to find new partnerships, programs, etc. to also help us grow. The first partnership I sought after was the Black Women's Networking Missouri/Illinois Chapter (BWN MO/IL). Black Women's Networking was launching their Missouri/Illinois Chapter this month and I was so excited to be a part of it. After researching the organization, I discussed becoming a business member with the Director of the Youth Development and Education program explaining that it would increase our network and elevate us to a new level. The Director agreed and I joined as a new Business Member. Although soon after joining, I wasn't quite sure how they would help elevate our program, other than increasing the awareness of who we are. It's safe to say that I didn't feel like Black Women's Networking Missouri/Illinois was for me and I didn't fully understand who they were or what they did. I was only concerned with increasing the Youth Development and Education program footprint. Although, the President of Black Women's Networking remained in touch with me and followed all my accomplishments even though I was not as present in the organization as I should have been. Throughout the rest of the Spring semester, the Youth Development and Education program continued to grow in students served, partnerships and projects. It's safe to say we had a very productive end to the school year.

Summer 2015 was quickly upon us and not only had I gone back to my roots and rejoined the Boys and Girls Club as a part of the staff to open a new location, I was about to marry the man of my dreams, and I was also inducted into the Boy's and Girl's Clubs of Greater St. Louis Hall of Honor. Here I was 32 years old, an educator, Executive Director, a Board Secretary, a Hall of Honor inductee and about to be a wife! Life couldn't get better than this could it?! We had a small ceremony that summer and planned to have our Big wedding a year later. See, I had lost my grandmother already and wanted to be sure my grandfather could witness my marriage so, with about 12 people, my husband and I were married at my cousin's house and then met our close friends and family to celebrate after. The highlight of our summer, marrying each other or so we thought. Soon finding out that we were pregnant topped everything. I know what you're thinking.? How did I find time to get married in the midst of all the jobs I had and now a baby? I made time. No matter how busy you are or what you have going on you must make time for the things that matter. For me, Love, wife, and motherhood have always been at the top of that list, so believe me when I say I will always make time and you should too.

Back to the books or shall I say the new school year crept upon us and it was back to business as usual. Although a few weeks into the fall I started having complications with the baby that ultimately resulted in a miscarriage. My husband and I were very devastated. My emotions were all over the place and at times it came out in all areas of my work. As a woman, it's very hard to hide your feelings and although I was advised to do so while at work, I opted to again Dare to be different, embrace that part of my journey and share it with my students, mentees, and coworkers. Which proved to be very therapeutic. After taking a little time off, I jumped back into my work and swore to show everyone what I was made of. See my husband and I prayed and asked God for understanding and the answer we received was that it wasn't our time yet. Very hard to accept but we had to in order to keep going. Jumping back into my busy life posed a lot of questions from the Director of the Youth Development and Education program when it came to some of the business decisions I was making. I started hearing, that's an emotional response or you made that decision based on your emotions instead of being focused on the business. What the Director didn't understand is that as an Educator of any kind your decisions are going to be very emotional when your main concern is the care and wellbeing of the students. Over the next couple of months, I helped create and implement Holiday service projects, Christmas parties, parenting workshops, and a student college trip. At the beginning of the new year, the president of Black Women's Networking Missouri/Illinois Chapter checked in with me as she had done often to congratulate me on all my accomplishments but to also invite me to a chapter meeting. I had only been to one since I joined so I agreed to come. Exactly a year after I joined, and this meeting was the beginning of a new sisterhood and mentorship. It's now safe to say they were exactly what and who I needed in my circle as I began to evolve.

It was February 2016; we were finalizing the details for the student College trip and I had been feeling sick over the last few days. I tried to chuck the feeling up to my sinuses acting up and focus on my Husband, my many jobs and by Big Wedding that was coming up in a few months, but it had gotten too bad and I needed to be seen by a doctor. Not wanting to wait any longer, I decided to take a day off and go to Urgent Care. Of course, as I assumed, I had a sinus infection but what I didn't anticipate was the Doctor telling me that I was pregnant! You read correctly; I was pregnant! I immediately began to cry and started making my phone calls in their office. The first phone call to my Husband to give him the news and the second to my OBGYN to confirm the findings. Two days later, we were at the Doctors office getting an ultrasound confirming that we were indeed pregnant and due October 2, 2016. We decided to keep our blessing to ourselves for a few weeks just to be sure everything was good. So, me, a Wife, soon to be mom, Educator, Executive Director, Co-Facilitator, and Board Secretary. Yeah, my life was about to be so busy and crazy, but I prayed on everything and knew these were all of God's blessings and he wouldn't put anything on me that I couldn't handle. Although, after disclosing my pregnancy, my decisions were again questioned, and it was said that my hormones were the reason I chose to do things a certain way. So, not needing to explain myself I chose to ignore the comments and continue. As we continued through yet another successful spring semester, increasing our reach and our footprint we added a social media presence that allowed our students to showcase their groups, the things they were learning and celebrate their accomplishments through the end of the year. This new presence also allowed our youth to spotlight, motivate and empower each other and others to new levels in their lives.

It was now time for my Big wedding/vow renewal weekend, and I couldn't wait, but that meant everything else had to take a back seat for about seven to ten business days. Now, you know since I had been making emotional/hormonal decisions according to others I knew there was going to be some backlash but being the woman that I am, I made sure to fully prepare for it. Before taking off, I made sure to have all paperwork, meetings, and classes set up for the next week so that no one could say anything about me being a woman and needed to take so much time off. As women, we choose to plan out and prepare for anything that may arise and I had done just that. So not one, not two, but all my positions were set up perfectly to run smoothly with no issues during my absence. Back at work a week later, I jumped right back into the fold as if I never left. The rest of that summer we prepared to teach our mentees some new curriculum in the fall all while my husband and I prepared for our new baby boy that was on his way in a couple of months. See being an Educator means no matter what your positions, who you work for or what you do, you will always be teaching and learning. Fast forward to October 2, 2016, our baby boy Kevin Joseph Arman II was born and life as we knew it was changed forever. Remember a couple of pages back when I told you that you always make time for the things that are important to you like love, being a wife and motherhood. Well, now that motherhood is officially put into the mix, the time that I put into everything immediately changes and my number one and two focuses are my Husband and my son, then everything else follows.

I had been on Maternity Leave for about 8 weeks and decided that I would go back to work a few weeks earlier. Originally planning on staying on leave for 12 weeks changed when our financial restraints changed. With a child, no matter how much you plan sometimes the finances are just not enough so you adjust accordingly. I went back to work as an Educator but explained to the Director of the Youth Development and Education program that I would not be coming back as the Executive Director and Co-Facilitator until after Christmas break which was the original plan. The Director said that he understood but in the same breath asked if I would put a one-sheet presentation together for him to use as a handout for a meeting. I agreed to do the sheet but quickly regretted it. Apparently, the hard work I put into the sheet he asked for was not enough and he was displeased, but instead of having a sensible conversation the negative response I received was very uncalled for and was the icing on the cake. Over the past couple of years, although I had done so much to help grow and elevate the program and parent company, I had received too many emotional and hormonal comments and I just couldn't take it anymore. After talking it over with my Husband, I ultimately decided to resign from being the Executive Director of the Youth Development and Education program and the Board Secretary for the parent company. In addition, I agreed to remain a Co-Facilitator for the Girl's program through May.

Coincidentally I also signed a new Wedding client in May. Yep, you read it right. A new Wedding Client. I know you're now reading and thinking where did this come from. Let me tell you. Growing up, my cousins had a Wedding Planning business, so they taught me everything they knew. During college, every now and then I would plan and coordinate Weddings and Events on the side, but I had gotten away from it for a while. Although after planning and coordinating my own Wedding I got the bug again and was referred to some new clients. Not really knowing what that meant for me at the time, but I would soon find out. Being an Educator means we get the summer's off so I would work at the Boy's and Girl's Clubs during that time. Well, this summer, being a new mom and signing a new client-led my Husband to tell me to take the summer off, enjoy

the baby and do something I always wanted to do. Little did he know that was one of the best gifts he would

have ever given me. Ever since I was a kid, I wanted to own my own business and he had just given me the

push I needed. That summer I went to several business seminars, enrolled in a business program and started my

first business, Moments When Dreams Come True Social & Corporate Event Planning on June 13, 2017. Here

again, having a lot of people in my ear telling me what I couldn't do, but also having the right people supporting

me and telling what I could do. Going through and completing the business program along with being

mentored by the president of the Black Women's Networking Missouri/Illinois Chapter guided me to a

successful start in business and beyond. By January of 2018, I was eighty percent booked up for the year and

counting according to the goal I had set for my first full year in business. You see Daring to be different will

have its challenges, but the rewards will overpower all of them.

Live to Inspire

Growing up, I was an at-risk youth and places like the Boy's and Girl's Clubs are a huge part of who I am

today, so it was only right for me to find a way to create those same opportunities. It was February 2018 and I

was finally ready to start my Youth organization. It was time for me to Live to Inspire. Living to Inspire meant

creating an organization to help our youth and families in the community. Initially, I always thought I needed a

building to get started but conversations with mentors and past, present and future support teams helped me

realize that I didn't have to have my own building to get started just a place where classes, sessions, and

workshops could take place. This is where Daring Inspired Youth was founded. We are a Youth Development

Consulting Firm who empowers youth to reach their full potential through character development classes,

mentorship, college & career readiness. We strive to provide a place where youth can express themselves as

they find their passion and explore it further. Encouraging creativity, which builds a well-rounded person. Our

sessions and workshops are held in the community at different locations throughout the city and state. We will

also come out into the community and come to your house as well as video chatting for our clients who are in other states and cities. Determined to touch as many youths as possible, we hold several events throughout the year. In addition to the workshops we offer, we partner with other youth groups to host teen nights, teen vision board parties, cooking classes, financial literacy workshops, a kidpreneur program, an annual youth gala where we give away awards, a five hundred dollar scholarship and donate a portion of the proceeds to a different youth organization every year, etc. This is how I Live to Inspire daily.

Be Who You Are

You know as you go through different trials and tribulations in life, let alone in business sometimes you begin to question exactly who you are as a person. Are you going through your everyday routine posing to be someone you're not versus presenting who you truly are? Sometimes you start off being yourself but get lost in the hustle and bustle of the world and slide into someone that you don't even know. Or maybe you're scared to know. You see, all my life I have always spoken to my peers about the things we go through and given advice whether I was a kid or an adult. I remember as a teen, talking to one of my mentors one day and her telling me I should take up public speaking. I laughed at her so hard and reminded her that I did not like public speaking, and she was talking crazy to me. She told me to always remember that conversation because at some point in life I would stop fighting one of my destiny's.

Throughout the years, believe it or not, I have always been a Motivational Speaker but I did it in smaller settings like workshops or training so when people would ask me to speak at an event I would shy away from it because I felt it wasn't the same. Although I just didn't want to admit it really was the same. Admitting it, meant acknowledging that public speaking was for me and a huge part of who I am. After multiple workshops, video recordings of myself speaking, meetings and small events, in January 2019, I decided to stop fighting the public speaking monster and embrace it instead. This is where I was no longer scared to show the world who I am. Committed to proactively create innovative methods of empowerment so that we may continue to approach our lives with self-confidence, Te'Ara Speaks, Motivational Speaker was born and is all about being who I am!

What is your biggest fear?

We all have fears that keep us from reaching our highest potential. What happened in your life that made you feel that you weren't worthy to reach your potential in business or even in your life?

Mompreneurship: Not for the faint of heart!

Let me encourage you.
by

Melanie Williams

Let me first define "Mompreneurship" as it relates to me: Taking on the added responsibility of starting and growing a business for the purpose of profit and teaching my children how to maintain the legacy I'm building to care for them and their children's children. While, at the same time, being an attentive, nurturing, loving, working, and sometimes tired wife, mother, sister, and friend. But don't let my definition deter you, this is my journey yours may be different. I just want to share with you some things I have learned that have helped me along the way. Parenting and starting a business for most entrepreneurs, especially mothers, for those I have asked, can bring about the same joys. You have your initial worries of course; can I do this? Will I be good at this? Will I mess up? But as the time for the delivery draws near most parents are just ready to meet the baby, see how it looks, whose personality it will have. You care for that baby and love it and nurture it and do all in your power to help your baby grow and be successful. When you have a business, you don't treat it any different, it's also like your baby. You love it and nurture it so that it grows. You hate to see it fail and you are proud of the milestones your baby and your business accomplish. In preparation for your baby, you often have special announcements involving family and friends and even co-workers. You throw parties where they shower you with gifts and words of encouragement. Some may even offer babysitting services and emotional support for days they know you will be down in the dumps with the occasional baby blues. Hey! Guess What! You do some of those same things for your business. You have marketing events where you introduce what you are doing to the world. You invite those same family members, friends and yes even coworkers to share in this special new moment. Never, not even once, thinking that the love and support will be any different for this "new baby" of yours than it was for the actual baby you birthed. Being an entrepreneur and starting your own business often bring about those same emotional baby blues when things aren't quite going the way that you had hoped. BUT that support you received IS MUCH different. The first thing you may have noticed but brushed off was the fact that not even everyone you invited came to celebrate you're being a business owner now. That emotional support hit different too! In fact, those closest to you, the ones who you think will be first in line to support you, will be the farthest from you when you need them near when it comes to matters of your "little business." Never did I understand scripture more than when I decided to try and include family in the processes of my business building. I found this especially true when it came to finances and why I thought having a family business was so important. Read if you will Mark 6:1-6 (v4)" But Jesus, said unto them, A prophet is not without honor, but in his own country, and among his own kin, and in his own house." **Sometimes we must create that separation, get** them around someone else saying the exact same thing for them to hear it. It's no secret that most people have a desire to see their loved ones do great things and be prosperous. But it's those same people who likely share this same desire that will treat you like the plague when you finally announce you've got a way to do it. They can't help it! If you can't see you doing better, you often can't see anyone close to you doing any better either. Now don't count this as a catch-all for those wanting to start a business. Some people have great support systems and it's a wonderful thing when you do. I just want to help the beginner who will be blinded by this if it happens and they aren't prepared. Not having this support often leaves many discouraged and for most, it brings the entire process to a dead halt. There are a select few who continue anyway. No matter where you fall, I want to encourage you. Whether you are just starting your entrepreneurial journey or you're continuing after a setback or two or three. First, I want you to know that this journey can be very rewarding if you keep your mind in a positive place through the ups and the DOWNS! Second, positivity is a process we often have to learn to practice THROUGHOUT the day. As strange as it may seem negativity comes to most people second nature! You can point out all the wrong someone has committed; you can spot a dead leaf before you spot the butterfly sitting right on top of it. Often, when we go through the processes of laying out our wants/desires, we often list what we don't want first because it's easier to conjure up the negative. We have to seriously ponder what it is we really want, and most of us still don't quite know. Our minds are powerful and what we think creates an energy that automatically sets us in motion affirming consciously or subconsciously what we give thoughtful attention to. Think now about how you see your life, business, relationship? Are you thinking about them in terms of growth? Or are you mulling over the pitfalls you've had? I have found this next sentence to be my sustaining growth sentence. YOU HAVE TO BELIEVE FOR WHAT YOU WANT OUT OF LIFE, BUSINESS, AND LOVE. You must have a mental picture of what that looks like and you must consciously view that mental picture several times a day. For this purpose, I have created a new vision board every year that I keep right up on the wall in front of my desk right above my computer. Whenever I am having some kind of mental blockage, I can look up at that vision which happens to be surrounded by pictures of my "why" and I can get myself back on track when there is no one there to kick me back in action. I have also taken a picture of my vision board and have used it as my screen saver on my phone. Sometimes that phone can be a distraction too, so seeing that picture on my phone gets me back on track. I started my entrepreneurial journey in grade school, not really understanding what I was even on the journey. First selling cookies and school supplies, then doing hair to help my mom purchase those very same things for me and my sisters, all the way into high school. I didn't see myself as an entrepreneur until well into college when I decided I wanted to publish some of my poetry and children's books and sell them. You know, become this well-known author, selling thousands no maybe even millions of books to support my parents and grandparents and my own children for centuries to come. All I needed to do was share that dream with those closest to my heart. Right?! So, I started with my closest family and friends, getting them to read my work and give me some critiques. Never mind several published professors have already done this. Needless to say, what you are reading now is my first published work. I was so taken back by the lack of support I was paralyzed in the process. I even managed to anger my now husband who swore that poetry written before I even knew him was about him. I was so confused and not prepared for all the negativity I had received, and I didn't know how to get that focus back. If my family and closest friends and loved ones were so NOT on board, how was this going to work?! Would I even sell a book? I had lost my "why" at that moment because my "why" couldn't see the clouds for the sky Thinking back now I wish I had realized that I was so good I got people in their emotions without even knowing their situations. Don't get me wrong I did have some folks cheering me on. "No! Go ahead and do it! Don't let them syke you out." But how many of you know we weigh the opinions of people differently even when we want to go forward. Ultimately, we must decide to commit to our decisions to do what it is we're going to do NO MATTER what someone else says and then we must be consistent in following the plan we've laid out to get there! Don't let people (family, friends or foe) from your "hometown" make you miss out on living your dream. It took me some soul searching and some stranger pressure to realize I have What's Up, so you can Wake Up, and get your Wealth Up! I have a talent given to me by God and it is in my writings. #IAmMelSpeaks   Years later I decided I'm going to do this entrepreneur stuff again. My true desire to be an involved mother/wife and leave the kind of bills my children's children could spend in my legacy is pulling at me more and more. I started an online resale shop. I was getting in good donations. I was getting a little bit of notice on the web and random calls were coming in wanting to know more about my business and what we had. I made a few sales, but I still hadn't hit that boom status yet. I had more support this time from family and friends they were donating, shopping and even helping a little with inventory and marketing. I was super excited! But I was still the head of all things that were running with my business, so when I was called to serve my country as I vowed to do, just a few short months after getting the business ball rolling, all my hard work came to a halt and when I returned 11 months later I was back to ground zero. If you never learn anything about going into business and what should be a part of your long-term strategy for growth LEVERAGE is your business staple. After many long nights of starting over, I started a separate business partnership with another businesswoman who went to my home church, it was in this business partnership that I was introduced to the concept of leverage and it was a light bulb moment for me. No one can build wealth alone! There are things and people that we all need to get to the next level we want, and we should seek those things and people and use them to the best of our abilities. Now "USE" is a word that gives people a bad taste. But that is because we are using the word NEGATIVELY! Remember what I said about mindset and how that negative thought is the quickest one to populate the mind. In Business, you need to use people for many things their talents and know-how are a big one. We understand this when we go apply to work for someone who will give us a salary, a few vacation days and a desk. Tell us when we can come, go, eat and be sick. But we don't understand this when that person is someone we know who just started a new business. For some reason, that person is no longer allowed to say I want to use you for your talents and know-how and this is what you will be paid, because "that's my friend". We have to, not only prepare ourselves for the abundance that learning about leverage can bring us but also the backlash we may get from those that still have no real clue of what it is and how they are already using it or being used by it every day. Leverage, as it relates to business, is simply borrowing of talents or resources or monies for gain. I say borrow because you can't take someone's talent you can only borrow it for as long as they allow you for whatever price/value they have placed upon it. Those who don't understand their talent have the hardest time dealing with leverage because they don't see how to put a value on what they have done or are doing for someone else, so they feel used. I can speak to this from personal experience. If there is something you do often that people compliment you on, or are always asking you to do often, take notice to that, you may well be working in your gift. Don't downplay it, grow in it and help those watching you grow in theirs as well. Talents are like money and because we all have them there is no reason for any of us to be in lack. In fact, for those who are believers, God says so. Read Matthew 25:14-30, we are supposed to go out and share those talents/gifts with others as this helps others to also realize and grow in their gifts/talents. I also had to learn this on my entrepreneurial journey. We can't be afraid to share the gifts and talents we have. No one will ever be able to outdo you in YOUR talent or gift. No one can steal your talent or gift. Many people share some of the same aspects as it relates to talent or gift, but no two people do it exactly the same. Operating in such fear is operating in a state of lack and that comes full circle back to that negative mindset. There is more than enough for everyone to get a piece and sharing opens doors for other pieces you may not have even realized you could use. Another major token I have learned to cherish on my journey is that I know my strengths and my weaknesses even when I don't care to share them or acknowledge them at the moment and for this reason, I think you should seek out an accountability partner who will be honest and straight forward with you. An accountability partner should be someone you trust and someone who believes in the vision you have for where YOU are trying to go because they will ultimately be responsible for keeping YOU responsible for all the actions or lack thereof in reaching your goals. This doesn't mean that a person has to necessarily be aligned with what your vision is they just need to be able to see what you want to do with the vision you have and you have to be able to trust that they will push you to do just that. But be warned, an accountability partner is NOT responsible for your successes YOU ARE! Take special care in knowing ALL advice, no matter how great it may sound, even when it's coming from someone who truly has your best interest at heart, is NOT FOR YOU!!! I learned this lesson by mistake, but it was a great lesson to learn because it has shown me my growth in knowing myself. I have 2 accountability partners; I trust them to do exactly what they have been assigned to do no matter how I take it! I chose two them because they both think outside of the box and they both think on different ends of the spectrum meaning they won't both give me the same advice, ideas or slack. Both of them have some awesome advice and for the most part, it has helped me to continue to propel myself forward through all the life happenings on this journey. But one piece of advice I was given just did not fit my way of working. It was GREAT advice just not for me. I was told to focus on getting one thing going great at a time. To keep the main thing the main thing and wait until that was going where I wanted it to go before starting on something else. At the time I was given that advice nothing was going quite where I wanted it to go as fast as I wanted it to so I was like: ok this must be why. I need to sit back and focus on one thing and then the rest of this stuff will better fall into place. NOPE, I tried so hard to focus on one thing that everything came to a halt! I do my best when I have "things" going on. I draw ideas for other projects in the projects I am already in. So, for me to focus on one thing was the punishment for my brain and creativity. Much of what I do can be traced back to something else I have done or am doing if that makes sense. For me, the main thing is ALL the things I was doing. I got back on my horses and I have been non-stop creating, developing and growing ever since with my accountability partners on my tails!! I LOVE IT!! So, to all my ladies on this journey, young and seasoned. I hope you can take this away from all that I have said: (1.) Your mind is GOLDEN! What you put into it is what actions come out of it. You have to get your mind right so that you can begin to your journey strong and finish stronger. (2.) Support is relative and YOU must be your biggest supporter, committed to your goal and consistent in the actions taken to reach that goal. This step is just as hard as step one and twice as important. Deadweight is a heavy load to carry and one of life's most popular distractions. A deadweight is often a person or people we have strong attachments to, we don't want to let them go no matter how apparent they have made it to us that they will not be a useful resource on this journey.

(3.) Leverage everything and everyone that you can, LEVERAGE is not a bad word. It is a resource. People and things can be resources! (4.) Get to know you! You have to know your strengths and weaknesses and be honest with yourself about them and USE them to your advantage! (5.) Get an accountability partner or two or heck as many as you need to help you stick and stay, choose them wisely and don't be afraid to NOT use all the advice you get from them. Like I said it may be great advice for someone just not for you. (6.) DO IT AFRAID!! Fear paralyzes success. If you're going to let fear stop you from doing something, let it stop you from quitting. Lastly, my own favorite quote "You can't help someone else more than you help yourself! You too are constantly learning throughout the process." I hope I gave you What's Up! So you can Wake Up! And get your Wealth Up! #IAmMelSpeaks #WhatsUpWakeUpWealthUp I hope to see you guys in front of the crowd!!

Girl Change your Attitude

By: Michele Sutton

Your attitude is everything, the way you act based on how you perceive the world. Google's definition is a settled way of thinking or feeling about someone or something, typically one that is reflected in a person's behavior. The saying "Angry black women" was a saying to make black women feel bad like we are the ones with the problem. "We always have an attitude." So, they say. Is it because we are so head-strong and speak with such confidence it's hard to find words to silence us? The fact is you are going to give attitude; my job is to show you the right attitude to give. Nobody owes you anything, but you can have anything you want. And if they do owe you, what about the ones that payback with interest? Isn't it a good feeling? To get back more than what you put in sounds like a loan in your favor. Life is a gift so you can't look at it as I'm getting what's owed to me. Look at is as I'm getting everything the devil thought he stole from me. For example, Tamera lost her dad when she was small to gun violence. Her mother started using drugs and it didn't take long for her to become an addict. She became a recovering addict and then an addict again. Despite Tamera's attitude people tried and wanted to help her. Not only because they felt sorry for her, but people genuinely believed if she put forth the effort, she could be great. Tamera burned every bridge with everyone. Nobody wants to deal with her anymore because she thinks the world owes her. The world does not owe her, and the world isn't going to pay her. God is going to pay her. This world will chew you up and spit you out; it is not for the weak. God gave your life! It is a gift! Yeah, life happened to her parents, now what can she learn from that? It doesn't have to be her. She shouldn't count herself out. How are you going to give back from what you learned? How can you serve him with the things he has given you? Empower others without giving yourself all the glory. Girl changes your attitude about yourself and loves you as nobody else can. Empowering and uplifting others is something you can do once you realize you are not perfect. When you see judging others and thinking you are better than the situation you are in. You must know that you are better than the situation you are in. You have to know that you can do better and deserve better. You start to mess up when you start getting confused thinking that you must be perfect and judging people is ok. Judging them like your sins and wrongdoings don't stink. Gina works in Corporate America and is the lead partner. She acts as if she never struggled with anything before and does not show compassion for others. As if everything she has was a birth-given right. Her way of empowering and inspiring others is telling them how good she is at working and if they work hard without expecting or getting handouts, they could be good too. She doesn't tell them to trust the process or even give thanks to anyone except herself. That will leave Gina lonely, friendless, and no one wanting to work under her. It's ok to be about your business at work, you are supposed to, and that is the business that pays you. But anybody that acts like that at work you can bet money they act that way at home. The same way God gives it to it can be taken away. Those same people that you once judged for needing handouts now you need them. Now you want to find them so they can lead you to some help. Change how you treat people love everyone; girl changes your attitude. You make the money don't let it make you. Don't settle for anything less than you deserve when it comes to business. Say what you mean and do exactly what you say you are going to do. People will value what you say when you do exactly just that. Don't get so caught up in money or the love of money that you forget about service or people. You are going to really like the things money gives you the opportunity to buy and do but don't let it consume you. Don't love money to the point you will do anything to get money. Don't confuse your wants with needs. Don't think you really need the things you can live without. If you can live without it don't go in debt, lose your home, or do anything to get it. As you grow you will see how pointless and crazy that was to do. For the love of money, people will steal from their grandmothers and sell their soul for an item that wouldn't even matter if they died right now. I understand you must eat, and I believe in being friendly but not free. Meaning everything is going to cost you. They say the best things are free like family and friends. But your family and friends may need something sometimes. All I'm saying is all money isn't good money. Does it spend? Sure, it does. At what price? My grandmother always said, "Don't just take money from anyone". She had seen firsthand what money can do to people. When she was a child, they almost lost everything due to a gambling habit her dad had and the things he would do for money. She saw how money could build you up and make you fancy but destroy you and leave you with nothing. A father she never really got a chance to know because of his love for money. Girl changes your attitude about money. You are in control and don't you forget it. If a man is intimidated by how strong you are or how you make things happen, do not dim your light to make him or anyone else feel comfortable. You are in control of your life! Not your past experiences, not that bitter friend, or angry mother. You are in control of you. Don't let anyone determine your attitude or how your life is going to go. Bad things are going to happen, and you are going to feel like you are losing control. At this point, you pray to whoever you believe in and just know you can get through it. Even If you are not religious you have to know life is worth living. If Jan loses control every time something happens in her life and needs someone else to tell her what to do Jan has a problem. Now there is nothing wrong with talking to a therapist, life coach, or spiritual advisor but even they are going to tell you to take some control of your life. Sometimes we don't want people in our business or even feel comfortable talking to others about our life. It is ok to talk to someone that gets paid to listen. You won't hear your business again in the street and you don't have to worry about them telling your family your business. If you keep things bottled in it can hurt, you. Letting go by speaking about it will give you relief. If your man is doing something that is bothering, you speak to him about it. Don't hold that in because it will eat at you. Once you speak about it to him you have done your part. Now he needs to do his part and fix it. Let him be the man, but don't lose yourself. If he is a man and I'm pretty sure at this point you know what a real man is, a provider and a protector. A man wants to feel like a man. It doesn't make you any less strong if you let him be the man. It gives him a sense of belonging and it shows him you want him around, even need him. The girl loves that man and is the woman. You have the power. Just because he is your man doesn't mean you have to turn into this perfect woman that forgets what makes her happy if he isn't involved. Having your companion there is always a plus, but before you got him you had days where you were happy or doing just fine, so don't put too much pressure on yourself it will ruin you and change your attitude. You don't have to get upset with him if you start to feel like you aren't the same you anymore. If you are messy don't add a significant other to your mess. Google's definition of messy when it comes to a situation is confused and difficult to deal with. You can't be a messy woman and expect a man or woman to clean it up. If you are difficult to deal with you need to know that you are. Don't lie to yourself by telling yourself, "It's them it's not me." Don't look at your partner crazy when he tells you that you are difficult especially if you know you are. Own it. That's what marriage is about knowing yourself while learning what works for your spouse. The more you know the better you guys can grow. But you can't grow if you aren't willing to change or willing to hear what someone else has to say. If you start to feel like you aren't the same you anymore and you don't like the person you are becoming you can always change but change for the better and the right reasons. Don't change because you want to be like someone else or because you think he wants you to be somebody else. Change because you want different or more. It is so easy to look at someone who has a lot and say I want that life. You have no idea what that person went through to get it or what they are going through now to keep it. Just ask people, some may share some may not. Don't assume it's easy and pain-free. The grass is not always greener on the other side no matter how green they say it is. You are going to change that's part of life nothing stays the same, but you can be you. At least once a week dedicate a day or some time just for you. If you can't do once a week because you are extremely busy, you definitely need to write some days down that you may be free and make sure monthly you are using those days to relax, free yourself or just decompress. How can you work on yourself and that attitude if you never take time out for yourself? I would have a bad attitude too.

Apologizing doesn't make you look weak. Apologizing shows that you are human. No one wants to be around someone especially someone that knows they are wrong but just must blame someone else. Like saying I apologize I was wrong is going to put them in a casket. Apologize to those in-laws that you cursed out because you thought they were disrespecting you. They don't know you as your family does, so explain it to them on a level they can understand. Talking to them this way shows them you can communicate when signals get crossed. Sometimes you must change the people around you. If your friends are single and you are the only one married, you may not want to discuss the marriage life with them. They can still be your friends, but you may want to get advice from a spiritual advisor or what I call a "seasoned wife" when you want to discuss marriage issues. A seasoned wife is a woman that has been married for many years and you know she is going to give you great advice because she tries to live right and do the right thing. Changing the people around you could be finding more business-minded friends or influential friends. I have friends that I have known since we were kids that I am still close with, but I probably wouldn't call all of them if I wanted to start a business. I am that inspirational friend that will try to inspire you to do all things. Everyone isn't like that. That doesn't mean their intentions aren't good it just means that's not who they are. Some people don't want to lead they rather follow. Following is ok if you know you are good at that. Who are you following? That is the question that you should always have when you decide to do it somebody else way and not yours. If I believe with all my heart that God is going to do what he promised. I'm going to follow his word. I'm not going to try to change his word because I don't want to follow anymore. Change yourself! Change your attitude.

Family, friends, and associates are sometimes just titles. Expecting everyone you ever looked out for to support you will kill you if you don't grasp hold of this concept. I don't care how long you knew her or that Johnny is your little brother everyone is not going to support you or even buy from your business. Now some people may say they will support you and have intentions of doing so but never do. You can't let that get in the way of how you handle business or how you treat people. You will have friends or co-workers that support you more than family. You will find strangers that believe in you more than people you have known your whole life. It's crazy how life works out that way, but you still do your part. Some people don't believe in things until you show them. Showing them that you can do something is motivation. Take it as that. Make people believe in you. Change the way you view people and that will help change your attitude.

Misery loves company. If your attitude is nasty 9 times out of 10 you know it because people already told you. Drama is either somewhere around you constantly, or no one is around you even willing to help you. When you have a negative view of the world without even knowing it's so easy to destroy yourself or ruin the person next to you. A child is going to take in everything around them. Everything they see and everything they hear will be something they try to do. If I'm always being negative around my child there is a chance my child is going to be a negative person. If I'm cursing and fighting around my child more than likely my child is going to try to do the same thing. We have to watch the way we speak to our children and people in general. Speak life! It changes the atmosphere. People will gravitate to you more when you are positive. Your children will be social with others in a positive way. That will help them grow and succeed. Have you ever had a bad day and you went around a person that spoke so positive to you it changed the way you were feeling about that day? Be that person. Change the way someone is thinking by speaking life and being positive. Misery loves company so if you don't rub off on the ones next to you, you will try to make someone as miserable as you. If your family doesn't talk to you because you bring everyone down, or you have no friends because you can't get along with anyone change your attitude. You will enjoy life a lot more when you check yourself and change your attitude.

Don't let this world shake you. Be in this world but not of it. Things are going to happen in life, you may gain it all, you may lose it all. Don't let the craziness of the world distract you from following your passion and completing the mission. We live, we die but what are you leaving behind? What kind of legacy do you want to be attached to your name? That is important to know. When I was younger no one talked to me about being financially free. I didn't take a class on being debt-free. I did hear a lot about being spiritually free. What I have grown to understand is that the two are bonded. To not go under in this world, you got to try to be debt-free. Stacy is going off to college and no one has taught her about saving money and staying away from credit cards unless you absolutely need, she may end up in financial trouble. The family around Stacy is already struggling with their debt so they can't help her financially, but they can talk to her about the mistakes they have made when it came to money. I understand Stacy may be one of those people that feel like she has to learn through trying and experience, but if you have someone telling you and showing you how they messed up let's take that into consideration when handling money. If we do it that way more than likely we can avoid letting that same thing happen to us. To be free wholeheartedly you have to be spiritually free. Don't let this world shake you. Every day will be a new adventure. Sometimes it will feel like it's always something. You must remember who you are during things. When life happens, it happens. This means you must be prepared for anything and there will be some things you won't be prepared for, but you must know how to handle it. If I lose everyone close around me, I'm going to hurt and be upset and that's ok. I must remember God has a plan for my life. He has a plan for your life. We can't dictate or determine when someone is leaving this world. We must play our part and love each other. Faith plays a major part when life hits you where it hurts. It's so easy to praise him when you are living your best life and everything is going well, but when things happen like it will do you still feel the same way? Or does your faith start to shift and your attitude changes and next thing you know you done forgot who you are and who bought you this far. There is a season, beginning, and an end to all things. You will grow and make necessary changes if you need to. The things you used to hold dearly may not mean so much as you grow. And the things you may careless about you may start to realize you need it more. The older you get your outlook on life changes. What you spend your time doing is more important, what and who takes in your space is important, what you eat, and drink is important. I love to eat and try new food, but what I'm learning is that I eat a lot of unhealthy food that I have passed down for my children to eat. I am trying to change the way I look at food. I want to eat to live and not live to eat. I am becoming more aware of the things that are hurting the people in my family like high blood pressure, stress, and stroke. We must be mindful of things that have happened to people before us and stop generational curses. Some of those things would be the things that we accept, how we do those things and the way we eat. We are talking about lifestyle changes so it will not be easy. Especially if your whole household is already the things you want to change. You should live every day like it's your last. Give it purpose. What do you want to be doing on that last day? Nobody wants to think about it, but you don't want to be that person that waited and said I wish I could have gone there or seen this. Change is exciting to some and scary for others. How do you feel about change? Can you adapt to it? Are you willing to change? What is important is making the change when necessary. If it's bringing you down, make the change. If you feel lost make the change. If you tired of doing the same thing, make the change. How do you make the change? It starts with you. You have to know there is a need for change. How do you know this? Life will show and tell you. If your doctor tells you that you need to stop drinking alcohol because it's affecting your liver and you are addicted. If you don't stop drinking life will probably show you that you should have stopped. Addiction is tricky and illness, so you have to be careful about how you approach it. We can get addicted to anything. Drugs, alcohol, sex, food, and people are a few addictions. People can get addicted to even stranger things or things I didn't even think to mention. The trick is to know when you are addicted or listen when someone says you may need to talk to someone about that. That's why I said early to be careful what takes up your time or gets in your space. It will consume you if you aren't careful. Sometimes our attitude gets in the way and it's hard to see ourselves especially if you have been hurt, betrayed, or felt broken. I truly believe everyone needs someone even when you think you don't. We weren't made to be alone if that was the case why you not on this earth by yourself? It doesn't matter how independent you are or who hurt you. You need a friend. Especially a friend that's going to tell you the truth rather you like it or not. I want the best for you and the best version of you. When you shine I do too? When you come up with new ways to make things better you pave the way for me too. If I see someone that looks like me doing something, I want to do it gives me hope and motivation. As my daughter grows, I want her to know she can do all things as the scripture says. Sometimes you need that motivation or that push. When you see someone else doing it you should support them and be inspired. We don't have time to be mad or worried about why someone has something you don't have. We all have the same 24 hours. Don't get confused with the saying bad things happen to good people. Life is what you make it. How are you going to spend the rest of your life? Not mad! So, what he left you, so what daddy wasn't there, so what your car broke down and you must ask people for rides. Be happy despite it. I have been there. I know it doesn't feel good when it's happening but when you look at life a little different and realize you could be in worse places it should make you smile a little more. You should feel blessed when you may have to walk a little more. Some people don't have legs to walk and they wish they could walk. When you go into this New Year and the new season of your life remember to check yourself and your attitude. If you have a check on yourself, you can handle everything else.

The Pearl that Roared

By: Temycka Carpenter

There nothing like being an entrepreneurial woman on the rise with a mission to globally expand worldwide. You have probably come across people that say being a woman is a gift and a curse, quite frankly I agree. However, certain circumstances arise and you begin to question your position in life. You begin to imagine how something described as a gift and a curse is so beautiful too now feels like a burden to be borne. Womanhood can generally be quite tasking and demanding even when you have to go at it with no manual, it can be very difficult. Possibly most of the fears expressed concerning being a woman are not unheard of.

A large percentage of these fears are real. It can be tough trying to maintain your mental health while juggling all the activities, thriving in your endeavors and of course taking proper care of the kid(s). It has been established that it isn't a walk in the park, but we must also state that it is entirely possible and in fact, most women express joy and fulfillment at being a parent.

There are quite a large number of women who are parents through the death of a spouse, divorce, abandonment or choice. While some of these women often feel like they have got it really rough, or that they are doing just about everything wrong; there are others who are successfully and joyfully raising children by themselves.

Society has overtime categorized mothers into a hierarchy of respectability depending on how they became mothers. Up the ladder of the hierarchy is the widowed mother who is pitied, followed by the divorcee who is given some kind of compassion. However, the single mother by choice is hailed for her revolutionary act, whereas in reality she is looked upon as incomplete. Further down the ladder are the single teen mothers who are seen as irresponsible, reckless, loose and unfortunate.

Being a single mom in this society isn't just a description but also a license for society to pass judgment on not just you but also on your children. Many children in the US and indeed all parts of the world are raised by moms and are doing exceptionally well. What they need from society is not judgment and stigma but support. Everyone has to understand that no matter the category of parenting, what is, most important is the love, dedication, and care given to the child to enable you to grow in a healthy competitive environment while building a powerful empire.

My name is Temycka Carpenter-Carlton better known as "The Momologist" and the founder of Divinity Devine LLC and The Locked Up Love Initiative Project as well as Women On The Rise Consulting.

I am a success and mindset coach for moms who want more. I help women who are mothers to stop putting themselves on the back burner so they can find their vision & purpose outside of motherhood to take action and create the mindset, confidence, and life they truly want for themselves whether it to start a nonprofit profit, write a book, start a business, or just plain go back to school, etc. while leaving a legacy to their children.

As well as helping Moms do Soul Healing so that they can realign their life & reconnect with the right support while mending relationships amongst their families balance after their child has been diagnosed with a learning & behavioral disability. I also globally empower women to rebound from emotional trauma and break the cycle of incarceration while reducing the negative impact of captivity after losing a loved one to incarceration.

I also provide Social Media Management services for online & or "brick & mortar" businesses with Marketing & Branding. I focus on posting the right content, FB/IG ads, engagement, generating leads building their audience (traffic) for Facebook, Instagram, Google+, Twitter & Pinterest, etc. I also help with the startup of logos, flyers, content creation, website building, and business cards and any of their printed marketing & branding materials for their business.

I am a certified life and relationship coach, and a single mother of five. I have an Associate's in Paralegal Studies and a Bachelor's in Behavioral Science and a Double Masters in Mental Health Counseling and Sports Exercise Psychology. I have been a Mompreneur for the last couple of years, running multiple businesses in industries ranging from digital marketing, coaching, consulting, and financial services.

I have been a Mompreneur for the last 10+ years running multiple businesses stemming from Digital Marketing & Social Media Management, Coaching, and Consulting allowing me to learn many skills and techniques to find my calling in life. By no means did I become successful overnight it took trial and error and a lot of being open to change and growth.

Coming from the bottom and having no clue how to even start a business and trusting the wrong people has created years of mentally feeling like I was all over the place. Until I started to surround myself with like-minded women who supported my dreams and vision and it started to become easier along the way. Venturing into business entrepreneurship was the farthest thing from my mind when I started my journey. It was just establishing a career that was going to help me become financially independent as well as provide my children with a peaceful life.

I found my calling in helping moms through the process of navigating the special education system because of my own experience of advocating for my son (now 14) and daughter (4) and my daughter (12). But by no means did I become successful overnight it took plenty of trial and error and a lot of being open to change and growth.

My journey began as a teenage mom who didn't go to prom or social gatherings and was judged because of the choice that was made to enter into motherhood. I struggled to make ends meet, juggling commission-based work-from-home jobs and dealing with a lot of medical issues, all while feeling sorry for myself. I struggled with feelings of inadequacy and that nothing I did was good enough. Eventually, I reached my breaking point and reality set in. Overwhelmed, exhausted, and falling deeper into debt, I had no time for my children and lost sight of what I wanted out of life. That's when my epiphany hit: I decided to become an entrepreneur and stop working for less than I was worth.

When my son started school and was labeled as having behavioral and academic issues, I went into denial. It was at that moment when I realized I couldn't do this alone and was introduced to a peer advocate. From that point on, I knew that having the right support was important in finding any type of emotional balance. My only son was struggling with everything he saw me going through. I needed to take care of myself in order to be a better mom to him and my other children.

So little old me a hustler, grinder, and motivator stood up and said, "I'm going to start another professional business for single moms like myself." I wanted to build a legacy for my children so they don't have to depend on anyone, so they will never feel like they have to stay at a dead-end job, and can live a comfortable and successful life on their own terms.

Although I was the first person to graduate college in my family, all I did was rack up a bunch of debt along the way. As the sole provider for my family, with five children and three disabled children to care for, entrepreneurship seemed like the best path moving forward.

My journey back into business began after I had a pulmonary embolism in November of 2012. I ended up getting sick again in February 2013 and had to relearn how to walk and eventually my business started struggling because I was doing everything alone with no team and that was a lesson in itself. I kept switching in between working for MLM companies and trying to rebuild my business at that time to make ends meet until I realized, why am I working for someone when I can work for myself in my business that I worked hard for? So, I entered into volunteer work for the court system that eventually led to working with parents who were in need of an advocate for their children. That then led me to work with school systems on their behalf to make sure their children were getting the right services they needed. I also started working and networking with a lot of single moms who were poverty-stricken and couldn't pay someone to help them get their lives back on track. I worked with them pro-bono to learn the laws, regulations, and services that these families needed until I implemented what I learned into my business to help these families and women to navigate through their life situations and relationships so they were able to start becoming more knowledgeable and aware of what going on outside of what they have been told by someone about their situation.

Within the world of entrepreneurship, there were a number of strategies that helped me get to where I am today. While mindset is part of it, without implementation, execution, and a solid plan in place, success in business and life is impossible. The key to mastering the work that needs to be done is to set attainable goals, create a supportive network system, let go of your past roadblocks, create a consistent routine, ask for help, readjust your priorities, reset your emotional boundaries, allow yourself to heal, allow yourself some time to grieve, and forgiveness from your flaws.

It was a struggle in the beginning because I had no set hours; I was working around my children's schedules, trying to set up as a legitimate business. I had to make sure that I had the proper documents for my clients, the right marketing material, a website, logo, software, and a business coach to help me through the process. Along with keeping my sanity in place so I didn't have a meltdown from all of the responsibilities that were on my plate every day while raising my children with no support system.

You might be thinking that it doesn't seem like a lot of work. I thought the same until I started working behind the scenes and saw the long hours it took to set up technology, create the right content, and engage my audience, and find time to implement and execute the services and products that my clients needed to help them to better their lives on a consistent basis while keeping my cool.

In my business, one of the strategies I used to scale my business is to not take anything personally. I learned that I am responsible for the relationships that I encounter and manifest in my business. As a business owner, you have to set the guidelines for what you will allow and what you won't allow. Remember, people are people and you should treat them how you want to be treated. It's easy to fall into the victim mentality, but you must start taking responsibility for the role you plays in your life and business. Think of your business as your baby: you cherish it and care for it, and it requires your full attention. So, always make sure that you have your ducks in a row as a business owner, just like you have managed to do as a mom.

The next strategy I used to scale my business was forgiveness. This is the hardest thing that most business owners and we as moms have to deal with on a regular basis. The truth is, forgiveness is not about letting someone off the hook. Forgiveness frees you and liberates you to move forward. It simply means that you have decided not to be trapped by the pain anymore. It is okay to forgive yourself for allowing yourself to be taken for a ride if that's what happened to you as well as forgiving yourself for doing too much or not enough. Make sure you forgive yourself for not being perfect because we all have flaws, and forgive yourself for choosing the wrong path. Its nothing like forgiving yourself for the million of other things you are beating yourself up over and just free yourself by forgiving yourself, and then move forward.

My business was created around a new and improved life of happiness and less drama after I started over. As scary as it sounds, starting over is the most freeing thing you can do for yourself and your children. You may have a plan or you may not (I recommend having a plan) but the point is that you can do life differently. You can go where you want to go, do what you want to do. Creating a new life is about living the way you always dreamed you would live. That doesn't mean your new life will be free of problems, but simply that you won't have the headaches and heartaches of repeating the nonsense you went through in your past. It allows you to be more available if you have more than one kid, to spend more quality one-on-one time with each of them. This will help you feel better when connecting with your kids and will make you feel more in control of the situation.

As a business owner, I mastered a unique and humbling way of surrounding my life around the organization both personal and professional. Keeping things organized can be especially tricky if you've got children in the home. You want to establish a good system so that going forward all of their schoolwork and all of your work materials have their own home. You must decide what you want, write down your vision or plans for your life, and take the first step towards achieving your goals. In order to get to that point in your life, you will need to change your way of thinking methodically and strategically. You have to wipe out the negativity and stop wasting energy on being angry, depressed and self-destructive. Instead, find the positive in everything and focus on it. It's hard at first, but it will get easier over time. Organization happens the longer you're in business; as long as you keep extensive notes and systems in place eventually your business will start to run itself.

Wouldn't it be huge if you could consistently put your needs first? This means eating properly, moving regularly, reading books, listening to life-affirming music, and resting properly (sometimes hard, but I always make it part of my routine). If you feel drained, sick and tired all the time, you cannot focus or be productive. Remember, you are in complete control of your life. Nobody can make you do something you do not want to do. In the same way, you cannot make anyone else do something they do not want to do. Learning this simple lesson will make life easier. When you let go of controlling behavior, you can be exactly who you want to be in life and in your business. You can only be a positive influence, mentor or adviser to people who actually want this from you.

Always having a negative account balance and constantly struggling to pay my bills and turning to the streets was no fun or the life I had envisioned for myself and it was showing in everything I was doing. Financial stability, emergency funds, and a plan was the last thing on my mind. I eventually had to get real with my financial situation when my whole world was crashing down from being evicted because of no fault of my own and being blindsided to the fact that the company I kept around was the ones that put me and kids in jeopardy for the gain of themselves. Having to start from scratch helped me ensure that I was making the right financial decisions, picking the right financial plans, budgeting and living within my means. I decided to stop running up debt trying to impress others. I put a doable plan in place that set me and my children up with the money for emergencies. I also adjusted my priorities, as I had to be both mother and father to my children.

When building a business and maintaining a family I never took out my frustrations on my children and most importantly never replaced my children with my work. Even though as moms sometimes we advocate for keeping the lines of communication open and talking it out, we have to realize that our child is neither our crutch nor therapist. You will not always see eye to eye. Accept the difference in opinions and move on. This helps your children begin to move on as well. It is important to let guilt, past, and bitterness go, so you can focus on the important things.

Building a community of supporters in the world of business will help you continue to spread your vision and mission. Do not be too proud or shy to call on people around you when you need their help or support. Don't isolate yourself from society. Take part in networking activities. Surround yourself with family and friends as much as possible who are supportive and believe in your vision and mission.

It was normal for me to embrace the challenges that I faced as a single mother and business owner. I was solely responsible for my household while still coming to terms with the changes that led me to that point, which transpired so quickly and unexpectedly. This process I was faced with in reality took time; months and even years for me to cope with and it blocked me from adequately providing emotional, financial, and material stability on a consistent basis to my children over time. I didn't fold and dwell on the past, I stayed positive and brave while breathing life into my children and their daily routines. My ability to cope with the situation at hand determined the outcome of how my household coped while I was running a business.

Healing was imperative when I decided to rebuild and focus on running a successful business. When I moved into the healing stage I pushed past the situation that had left me as a single mom. I refused to let others tell me how I should feel. I was always reminded that I needed to experience that pain, those emotions, all in my own time. It was no question that I needed to work through a lot of it without focusing on healing all of the time. The distractions that were set in place were going to a movie, dinner, reading a good book, listening to music, or even packing for a trip.

It's so frustrating that as a society we work so hard and have no clue how many moms exist around us. I struggled with being left alone to raise my children while their father was in and out of the prison system, deemed a 3x repeat felon. I was taking bus rides every weekend to see him, trying to make sure he had food, money on the phone, letters … all while taking care of my family and neglecting myself. That's when I got sick and realized I was killing myself for him. It came down to this: did I put me and my household first, or keep chasing a one-sided life? And I chose me. No man was worth my sanity or my health or a chaotic household.

The moral of the story is I left myself vulnerable. And when all is said and done, I had to take care of me in order to be my best for my children. That meant cutting my losses and now I'm WINNING. You can too! The truth can hurt, but it doesn't have to hurt alone. So if you're READY and willing to do the work, then make it happen and take advantage of the resources around you in order to live a healthier and more balanced life.

When you choose to live out a dream, you need a plan to make it come true. Once you have a plan, it is crucial that you ask for help so, what can you stick to it and get around any obstacles in your way. The inspirational pathway to my success was my late grandmother and great-grandmother. They always instilled in me to never settle, to always push through, be the best at whatever I do in life and never depend on anyone. I know they are looking down on me proudly. I am creating a legacy for my children so they can see that the sky's the limit to your dreams when you work hard and grind your way to the top.

When I am feeling discouraged, exhausted, or like giving up, I go to the gravesites of my grandmother and uncle (who was like a mother and father to me) to talk to them or cry to them from the comfort of my house. Along with meditating and praying, these things allow me to bounce back because I know they hear me. Faith has definitely kept me on the right path while experiencing numerous trials and triumphs in my businesses ready to give up and just throw in the towel.

The fight every day for creating a legacy for my children hits home for me. As someone who advocates for their children and other people's children no matter the circumstances. It helped my business prosper because I started to take care of myself, and stay organized. But what really you should take head to as you read this is that *"The truth is, forgiveness is not about letting someone off the hook. Forgiveness frees you and liberates you to move forward. It simply means that you have decided not to be trapped by the pain anymore. Forgive yourself for allowing yourself to be taken for a ride if that's what happened. Forgive yourself for doing too much or not enough. Forgive yourself for not being perfect. Forgive yourself for choosing the wrong path. Forgive yourself for the million other things you are beating yourself up over. Free yourself by forgiving yourself, than move forward."* It is being able to let go of the pain, anger, and trauma that allows you to enable within a fresh start. It took me many years to learn this, but this piece of advice has also been integral to my own success.

When I began creating a new and improved life I started over in so many ways and had to shift my mentality to reflect the direction I was going in vs. where I was in life. As scary as it sounds, starting over was the most freeing thing I did for myself and my children. Having a plan in place and doing things in life differently has created a new life for me that I never could have imagined it allowed me to be more available for myself and my children. Once I became a business owner my life changed drastically I created time freedom, financial freedom, and that changed my life and it opened so many opportunities that were presented and opened the doors for me and my business.

My triumphs, as a Single Mom were tricky because my children got into everything and I had to establish an organizational system so that going forward all of their school work and my work materials had a home. This worked wonders because I was less stressed out and was able to methodically and strategically change the way I implemented the plans and vision of my business. I had to wipe away the negativity and stop wasting time and energy on being angry, depressed and self-destructive because it took time away from me running a successful business. So I found the positive in everything that brought me happiness and focused on that part of my business and let it run itself with the right systems in place.

When taking care of myself, my children, and the business I started to eat properly, move regularly, read books, listen to life-affirming music, and rest properly so my mind wasn't on overload and in a better space to make the necessary changes that I needed in life. The mere fact is that we are in control of our lives and can't anybody make you do anything that doesn't warrant a reaction. Learning this lesson will make life easier. When you let go of the controlling behavior, you can be exactly who you want to be. Learning self-control is something that will help you achieve success in your business and life. So, in essence, when you take care of yourself it allows you to take care of others clearly and in a way that is beneficial for all parties' advancement in life.

As a Single Mom, it required that I plan for the unexpected with first aid kits, and equip myself with the knowledge of allergens that caused an anxiety mindset around being and staying broke while trying to build a business. As well as prepare my children with emergency speed dials so they know who to call in case of emergencies when a financial crisis happens. Adjust some priorities as this is inevitable as I am both mother and father to my children as we financially started budgeting money towards what is the most important difference.

Being a woman in business in this new era is amazing because it shows society how far we have come as people. There was a time that women didn't run businesses let alone have a voice to stand on. It was a yes sir, no ma'am type of environment where we were seen as slaves. I'm here to let yall know that no matter where you are in life you can run a successful business of your choice through working hard and helping others while staying true to the vision and path you want. It will pay off in the long run. So, never give up keep moving forwarded and growing with the process to be the best entrepreneur possible. Your time is now and your journey is today.

NOTHING MATTERS MORE THAN THE PASSION IN YOUR HEART"

Sherika Mitchell Stroud

MILLIONAIRE
BOSS LADY
PLANNER 2020

NAME

BUSINESS

Simply write your 2020 Main Object Goal here. Once
you decide your goal, write out the phases on goal
phase, and when you plan to start and finish each phase.
Use the extra space if you need it! Good Luck Millionaire
Boss Lady!

Boss Goals	Starting	Ending		Boss goals	Starting	Ending

JANUARY	FEBRUARY	MARCH	APRIL	MAY	JUNE
S M T W T F S	S M T W T F S	S M T W T F S	S M T W T F S	S M T W T F S	S M T W T F S
1 2 3 4	1	1 2 3 4 5 6 7	1 2 3 4	1 2	1 2 3 4 5 6
5 6 7 8 9 10 11	2 3 4 5 6 7 8	8 9 10 11 12 13 14	5 6 7 8 9 10 11	3 4 5 6 7 8 9	7 8 9 10 11 12 13
12 13 14 15 16 17 18	9 10 11 12 13 14 15	15 16 17 18 19 20 21	12 13 14 15 16 17 18	10 11 12 13 14 15 16	14 15 16 17 18 19 20
19 20 21 22 23 24 25	16 17 18 19 20 21 22	22 23 24 25 26 27 28	19 20 21 22 23 24 25	17 18 19 20 21 22 23	21 22 23 24 25 26 27
26 27 28 29 30 31	23 24 25 26 27 28 29	29 30 31	26 27 28 29 30	24 25 26 27 28 29 30	28 29 30
				31	

JULY	AUGUST	SEPTEMBER	OCTOBER	NOVEMBER	DECEMBER
S M T W T F S	S M T W T F S	S M T W T F S	S M T W T F S	S M T W T F S	S M T W T F S
1 2 3 4	1	1 2 3 4 5	1 2 3	1 2 3 4 5 6 7	1 2 3 4 5
5 6 7 8 9 10 11	2 3 4 5 6 7 8	6 7 8 9 10 11 12	4 5 6 7 8 9 10	8 9 10 11 12 13 14	6 7 8 9 10 11 12
12 13 14 15 16 17 18	9 10 11 12 13 14 15	13 14 15 16 17 18 19	11 12 13 14 15 16 17	15 16 17 18 19 20 21	13 14 15 16 17 18 19
19 20 21 22 23 24 25	16 17 18 19 20 21 22	20 21 22 23 24 25 26	18 19 20 21 22 23 24	22 23 24 25 26 27 28	20 21 22 23 24 25 26
26 27 28 29 30 31	23 24 25 26 27 28 29	27 28 29 30	25 26 27 28 29 30 31	29 30	27 28 29 30 31
	30 31				

THE PURPOSE PRAYER:

Before I ask you for anything, I want to tell you thank you for life thank you for strength thank you for health thank you for allowing me to operate in my purpose. Sometimes it's not easy to understand who I am in a world that has a hard time defining what I'm supposed to do. I pray each day that my path is lit with love my way be made plain with understanding my hope to be built on faith family and trust.

I pray that all negative thoughts comments concerns and fears leave my mind and my heart. I speak clean and pure energy each day that I wake up in purpose.

Guide me as I elevate in both mind body and spirit cover me as I make humanistic mistakes forgive me as I era like only I can I pray for my sisters who want to live on purpose give them strength give them love and give them patience

Love peace and purpose

Written By: Sherika M. Stroud

Passion Points

What are 3 Things you are Passionate about?

☞ ____
☞ ____
☞ ____

Why are these things so important?

Make this moment your time!

Decree over your business and life:

- ❖ I am a millionaire.
- ❖ I am my own woman, in my business and in my life!
- ❖ I am every woman. I keep my sisters' heart, and love!
- ❖ I am a force to be reckoned with!
- ❖ I am who my creator designed me to be!